TOP **10**
BARCELONA

ANNELISE SORENSEN
RYAN CHANDLER

DK

EYEWITNESS TRAVEL

Left **Interior, Casa Lleó Morera** Right **La Rambla**

LONDON, NEW YORK,
MELBOURNE, MUNICH AND DELHI
www.dk.com

Produced by Departure Lounge, London
Printed and bound in China by Leo Paper Products Ltd
First American Edition, 2002

Published in the United States by DK Publishing, 345
Hudson Street New York, New York 10014
14 15 16 17 10 9 8 7 6 5 4 3 2 1

**Copyright 2002, 2014 © Dorling Kindersley
Limited, London
Reprinted with revisions 2004, 2005,
2006, 2008, 2009, 2010, 2011, 2012, 2013, 2014**

Published in the UK by Dorling Kindersley Limited.

A catalog record for this book is available
from the Library of Congress.

ISSN 1479-344X
ISBN 978-1-46540-998-0

Within each Top 10 list in this book, no hierarchy of
quality or popularity is implied. All 10 are, in the editor's
opinion, of roughly equal merit.

Floors are referred to throughout in accordance
with British usage; ie the "first floor" is the
floor above ground level.

MIX
Paper from
responsible sources
FSC™ C018179
www.fsc.org

Contents

Barcelona's Top 10

Cover: Front – **Corbis:** Sylvain Sonnet bl; **Superstock:** Axiom Photographic Limited main. Spine – **DK Images:**
Mike Dunning b. Back – **DK Images:** Max Alexander c; Naomi Peck cr; Paul Young cl.

Left **Jardins Mossèn Jacint Verdaguer** Center **CosmoCaixa** Right **Terrace café, Barri Gòtic**

Around Town

Streetsmart

Left **Plaça de Sant Felip Neri, Barri Gòtic** Right **Stained-glass ceiling, Palau de la Música Catalana**

Key to abbreviations
Adm admission charge payable **DA** disabled access

3

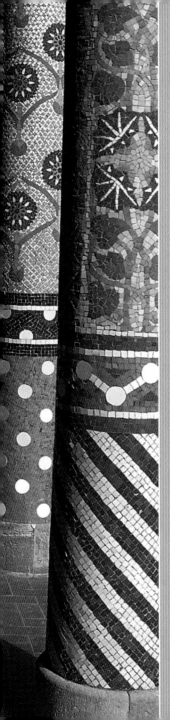

BARCELONA'S TOP 10

TOP 10 Barcelona's Highlights

With warm, crystal-clear waters lapping its sandy shores and mountains nuzzling up to its northern edge, this glittering jewel in the Mediterranean is blessed with desirable geographical genes. From the buoyant, revamped port area to the atmospheric medieval streets of the Barri Gòtic and the beautiful Modernista buildings of the Eixample, Barcelona has it all. A host of treasure-filled museums, architectural wonders, lively beaches and enchanting squares provide the icing on the cake.

Sagrada Família
The enduring symbol of the city and its *Modernista* legacy is this basilica, Gaudí's other-worldly *pièce de résistance*. Piercing the Barcelona skyline are eight of the 18 planned spires *(above)* that have so far been built. *See pp8–10.*

La Rambla
Barcelona's centrepiece, this 1-km-(0.6-mile-) long, thriving pedestrian thoroughfare *(above)* cuts a wide swathe through the old town, from Plaça de Catalunya to the glistening Mediterra–nean. *See pp12–13.*

Barcelona Cathedral
Dominating the heart of the old town is this magnificent Gothic Cathedral *(above)*, with a soaring, elaborate façade and a graceful, sun-dappled cloister containing palm trees and white geese. *See pp14–15.*

Parc de la Ciutadella
A verdant oasis in the city centre, Barcelona's largest park is criss-crossed with pleasant paths. It boasts a zoo, a lake and a lavish fountain *(right)*. *See pp16–17.*

5 Museu Nacional d'Art de Catalunya

The stately Palau Nacional *(right)* is home to the Museu Nacional d'Art de Catalunya (MNAC), which holds one of the most extensive collections of Romanesque art in the world. The works were rescued from churches around Catalonia in the 1920s. *See pp18–19.*

6 La Pedrera

Unmistakably Gaudí, this *Modernista* marvel *(below)* seems to grow from the very pavement itself. Fluid and eerily alive, its curving façade sprouts writhing wrought-iron balconies. A cluster of mosaic chimneys keeps watch over the rooftop like shrewd-eyed knights. *See pp20–21.*

7 Fundació Joan Miró

An incomparable blend of art and architecture, this spacious museum, awash with natural light, showcases the work of Joan Miró, one of Catalonia's greatest 20th-century artists. Paintings, sculptures, drawings and textiles represent 60 prolific years. *See pp22–3.*

8 Museu Picasso

Housed in a medieval palace complex, this museum charts Picasso's rise to fame with an extensive collection of his early works, including numerous masterful portraits painted at the age of 13. *See pp24–5.*

9 Palau de la Música Catalana

No mere concert hall, the aptly named Palace of Catalan Music *(left)* is one of the finest, and most exemplary, *Modernista* buildings in Barcelona. *See pp26–7.*

10 Museu d'Art Contemporani & Centre de Cultura Contemporània

The city's gleaming contemporary art museum *(above)* and it's cutting-edge cultural centre have sparked an urban revival in the El Raval area. *See pp28–9.*

🔟 Sagrada Família

Nothing prepares you for the impact of the Sagrada Família. A tour de force of the imagination, Antoni Gaudí's church has provoked endless controversy. The church was only partially complete when Gaudí died in 1926 and, as a work in progress, it offers the unique chance to watch the eighth wonder of the world in the making. During the last 80 years and at incalculable cost, sculptors and architects have added their own touches to Gaudí's dream. Now financed by over a million visitors each year, it is estimated the project will be complete by 2026, the 100th anniversary of Gaudí's death.

Passion Façade

🟢 Sit in a terrace bar on nearby Avinguda Gaudí and drink in the view of Gaudí's masterpiece illuminated at night.

🔵 For the best photos, get to the temple before 8am: the light on the Nativity Façade is excellent and the tour buses haven't yet arrived.

Look out for the cryptogram on the Passion Façade, where the numbers add up to the age of Christ at his death.

• Entrances: C/Marina (for groups) & C/Sardenya
• Map G2 • 93 207 30 31
• Metro: Sagrada Família
• Open: 9am–6pm daily (Apr–Sep: to 8pm)
• Adm: €13.50 (€18 with guided visit/audioguide); €17 for combined ticket with Casa-Museu Gaudí (€21.50 with guided visit/ audioguide)
• Guided tours: 11am, 1pm, 3pm daily (May– Oct & wknds: also noon)
• Limited DA

Top 10 Features

1. Nativity Façade
2. Passion Façade
3. Spiral Staircases
4. Spires
5. Hanging Model
6. Nave
7. Rosedoor Cloister
8. Crypt Museum
9. Apse
10. Unfinished Business

1 Nativity Façade
Gaudí's love of nature is visible in this façade *(above)*. Up to a hundred plant and animal species are sculpted into the stone, and the two main columns are supported by turtles.

2 Passion Façade
Started in 1978 and completed in 2002, this façade by Josep Subirachs represents the pain and sacrifice of Jesus. The difference between the Gothic feel of Subirachs' style and the intricacy of Gaudí's original work has not been without polemic.

3 Spiral Staircases
These helicoidal stone stairways, which wind up the bell towers, look like snail shells. They allow access to the towers.

4 Spires
For a close-up look at the gargoyles and mosaic tiling on the spires *(left)*, scale the bell tower stairs – or ride up in a lift. The views are equally spectacular *(see p55)*. Not for sufferers of vertigo.

For more churches in Barcelona See pp38–9

5 Hanging Model

This bizarre contraption in the crypt museum is testimony to Gaudí's ingenuity. Gaudí created this 3D construction – made of chains and small weighted sacks of sand – as a model for the arches and vaulted ceilings of the Colonia Güell crypt. No-one, in the history of architecture, had ever designed a building like this.

Sagrada Família Floor Plan

6 Nave

The immense central body of the temple (left), now complete, is made up of leaning, tree-like columns with branches spreading out across the ceiling. Inspired by towering redwood trees, the overall effect is that of a beautiful stone forest.

7 Rosedoor Cloister

In the only cloister to be finished by Gaudí, the imagery is thought to be inspired by the anarchist riots that began in 1909 (see pp30–31). The devil's temptation of man is represented by the sculpture of a serpent wound around a rebel.

9 Apse

Adorned with lizards, serpents and two gigantic snails, the apse was the first section of the temple to be completed by Gaudí.

10 Unfinished Business

The church buzzes with activity: sculptors dangle from spires; stone masons carve huge slabs of stone; and cranes and scaffolding litter the site. Observing the construction in progress (left) enables visitors to grasp the monumental scale of the project.

8 Crypt Museum

Gaudí now lies in the crypt, and his tomb is visible from the museum. Renovated to include audio-visual exhibits, the museum offers information about the temple's construction. The highlight is the maquette workshop, producing scale plaster and stone models for the ongoing work.

Sight Guide

The entrances to the Sagrada Família are on C/Sardenya and C/Marina (groups only) along with gift shops and lifts. There are two lifts, one in each façade, and they cost €4.50 to use (the stairs are not open to the public). The museum is near the entrance on c/Sardenya. Eight of the 18 planned towers are built, four in each façade.

For more sights in the Eixample See pp102–5

Left **Spiral staircase** Right **Detail of doorway, Passion Façade**

Key Sagrada Família Dates

1882
The first stone of the Sagrada Família is officially laid, with architect Francesc del Villar heading the project. Villar soon resigns after disagreements with the church's religious founders.

1883
The young, up-and-coming Antoni Gaudí is commissioned as the principal architect. He goes on to devote the next 40 years of his life to the project: by the end he even lives on the premises.

1889
The crypt is completed, ringed by a series of chapels, one of which is later to house the tomb of Gaudí.

1904
The final touches are made to the Nativity Façade, which depicts Jesus, Mary and Joseph amid a chorus of angels.

1925
The first of 18 bell towers, 100 m (328 ft) in height, is finished.

1926
On 10 June, Gaudí is killed by a tram while crossing the street near his beloved church. No-one recognizes the city's most famous architect.

Stained-glass window

1936
The advent of the Spanish Civil War brings construction of the Sagrada Família to a halt for some 20 years. During this time, Gaudí's studio and the crypt in the Sagrada Família are burned by revolutionaries, who despise the Catholic church for siding with the nationalists.

1987–1990
Artist Josep Maria Subirachs (b.1927) takes to living in the Sagrada Família just as his famous predecessor did. Subirachs completes the statuary of the Passion Façade. His angular, severe and striking sculptures draw both criticism and praise.

2000
On 31 December, the nave is at long last declared complete.

2010–2026
The interior of the church is completed, and in November 2010 Pope Benedict XVI consecrated it as a basilica. The completion of the entire Sagrada Família is forecast for 2026. The building of the Sagrada Família – as Gaudí intended – relies on donations. With so many paying visitors pouring in daily, construction work is gaining momentum.

For more on Modernista *architecture* **See pp32–3**

Top 10 Gaudí Sights in Barcelona

Antoni Gaudí

A flag bearer for the late 19th-century Modernista *movement, Antoni Gaudí is Barcelona's most famous architect. A devout Catholic and a strong Catalan nationalist, he led an almost monastic existence, consumed by his architectural vision and living in virtual poverty for most of his life. In 2003 the Vatican opened the beatification process for Gaudí, which is the first step towards declaring his sainthood.*

Chimneypot, Casa Vicens

Gaudí's extraordinary legacy dominates the architectural map of Barcelona. His name itself comes from the Catalan verb gaudir, *"to enjoy", and an enormous sense of exuberance and playfulness pervades his work. As was characteristic of* Modernisme, *nature prevails, not only in the decorative motifs, but also in the very structure of Gaudí's buildings. His highly innovative style is also characterized by intricate wrought-iron gates and balconies and* trencadís *tiling.*

Antoni Gaudí (1852–1926)

Trencadís Tiling

Gaudí's revolutionary use of *trencadís* tiling, a decorative art form which consisted of smashing up ceramics and piecing them back together in mosaic patterns, is particularly prevalent at Parc Güell. Another fine example of this technique is the rooftop of La Pedrera where some of the chimneys were tiled using hundreds of broken *cava* bottles.

Trencadís-tiled lizard, Parc Güell

⊓10 La Rambla

There may be no better place in the country to indulge in the Spanish ritual of the paseo (stroll) than on this wide, pedestrian street that is anything but pedestrian. An orgy of activity day and night, La Rambla is voyeuristic heaven. Spraypainted human statues stand motionless among the passing crowds; buskers croon crowd-pleasing classics; caricaturists deftly sketch faces; bustling stalls create an open-air market of bright bouquets and souvenirs; and round-the-clock kiosks sell everything from The Financial Times to adult videos.

Street performer

🔵 Kick back at the Cafè de l'Òpera at No. 74 *(see p42)* and soak up the Rambla ambience with a cool *granissat* (crushed ice drink) in hand.

🔴 Beware: La Rambla is rife with pick-pockets.

• Map L2–L6 • Metro: Catalunya; Liceu; Drassanes • Gran Teatre del Liceu: open for self-guided visits at 11:30am, noon, 12:30pm and 1pm daily (€5.50); guided tour of main building: 10am (€11.50); guided back-stage tour: 9am (€12.50), booking in adv essential; box office: open 1:30–8pm Mon–Fri, one hour before the performance Sat & Sun • Mercat de La Boqueria: open 8am–8pm Mon–Sat • DA
• Palau de la Virreina: galleries open noon–8pm Tue–Sat; usually free; Cultural Information Centre open 10am–8:30pm daily • DA • Arts Santa Mònica: open 11am–9pm Tue–Fri, 11am–2pm & 4–8pm Sat; free
• Església de Betlem: open 8am–1:30pm & 5:30–8pm daily

Top 10 Attractions
1. Gran Teatre del Liceu
2. Monument a Colom
3. Mercat de La Boqueria
4. Flower Stalls
5. Font de Canaletes
6. Miró Mosaic
7. Palau de la Virreina
8. Arts Santa Mònica
9. Bruno Quadras Building
10. Església de Betlem

Gran Teatre del Liceu
The city's grand opera house *(above)*, founded in 1847, brought Catalan opera stars such as Montserrat Caballé to the world. Twice gutted by fire, it has been fully restored.

Monument a Colom
Pointing resolutely out to sea, this statue *(above right)* of Christopher Columbus (1888) commemorates his return to Spain after discovering the Americas. An elevator takes visitors to the top for sensational views *(see p54)*.

Mercat de La Boqueria
A cacophonous shrine to food, this cavernous market has it all, from stacks of fruit to suckling pigs and writhing lobsters.

Flower Stalls

La Rambla is teeming with life and things to distract the eye. Amid the here-today-gone-tomorrow street performers and tourists, the true Rambla old-timers are the flower stalls that flank the pedestrian walkway. Many of the stalls have been run by the same families for decades.

Font de Canaletes

Ensure your return to the city by drinking from this 19th-century fountain, inscribed with the legend that anyone who drinks from it "will fall in love with Barcelona and always return".

La Rambla

Miró Mosaic

Splashed on the walkway on La Rambla is a colourful pavement mosaic *(above)* by Catalan artist Joan Miró. His signature abstract shapes and primary colours unfold at your feet.

Palau de la Virreina

This Neo-Classical palace was built by the viceroy of Peru in 1778. The Palace of the Viceroy's Wife, as it translates, is split into several galleries, showing mainly photography exhibitions.

Arts Santa Mònica

Once the hallowed haunt of rosary beads and murmured prayers, this former 17th-century monastery was reborn in the 1980s. Thanks to a massive government-funded facelift, it is now a cutting-edge contemporary art centre. Temporary exhibitions run the gamut from large-scale video installations to sculpture and photography.

Bruno Quadras Building

Once an umbrella factory, this playful, late 19th-century building *(left)* is festooned with umbrellas.

Església de Betlem

A relic from a time when the Catholic Church was rolling in pesetas (and power), this hulking 17th-century church is a seminal reminder of when La Rambla was more religious than risqué.

For sights in El Raval See pp80–83

Barcelona Cathedral

From its Gothic cloister and Baroque chapels to its splendid, 19th-century façade, the Cathedral, dating from 1298, is an amalgam of architectural styles, each one paying homage to a period in Spain's religious history. Records show that an early Christian baptistry was established here in the 6th century, later replaced by a Romanesque basilica in the 11th century, which gave way to the current Gothic Cathedral. This living monument still functions as the Barri Gòtic's spiritual hub.

Main entrance

🟢 Bask in the Cathedral's Gothic glory at the Estruch café on Plaça de la Seu.

🟠 Organ and choral concerts are usually held monthly; enquire at the Pia Almoina. Watch *sardanes* – Catalonia's regional dance – in Plaça de la Seu (6pm Sat, noon Sun).

• Plaça de la Seu • Map M3 • 93 342 82 62 • Metro: Liceu, Jaume I • Cathedral: 8am–12:45pm (to 1:45pm Sun), 5:15–7:30pm daily (until 8pm Sat & Sun); church and cloister free access, rooftops (via lift) €2.50, choir €2.50; guided tours (inc choir, rooftops and museum) 1–5pm daily (from 2pm Sun) €6 • Casa de L'Ardiaca: open 9am–8:45pm Mon–Fri, 9am–1pm Sat (Jul & Aug: 9am–7:30pm Mon–Fri); free • Museu Diocesà: open 10am–2pm & 5–8pm Tue–Sat, 11am–2pm Sun; €6 • DA

Top 10 Features

1. Main Façade
2. Choir Stalls
3. Cloister
4. Crypt of Santa Eulàlia
5. Capella del Santíssim Sacrament i Crist de Lepant
6. Capella de Sant Benet
7. Capella de Santa Llúcia
8. Nave & Organ
9. Pia Almoina & Museu Diocesà
10. Casa de L'Ardiaca

Main Façade
Flanking the entrance of the 19th-century façade *(right)* are twin towers, *Modernista* stained-glass windows and 100 carved angels. An eight-year restoration was completed in 2011.

Choir Stalls
The lavish choir stalls (1340), crowned with wooden spires, are decorated with colourful coats of arms *(left)* by artist Joan de Borgonya.

Cloister
Graced with a fountain, palm trees and roaming geese, the cloister dates back to the 14th century. The mossy fountain is presided over by a small, iron statue *(right)* of Sant Jordi (St George).

For more churches in Barcelona See pp38–9

4 Crypt of Santa Eulàlia

In the crypt's centre lies the graceful alabaster sarcophagus (1327) of Santa Eulàlia, Barcelona's first patron saint. Reliefs depict her martyrdom.

5 Capella del Santíssim Sacrament i Crist de Lepant

This 15th-century *capella* (chapel) features the Crist de Lepant, which, legend has it, guided the Christian fleet in its 16th-century battle against the Ottoman Turks.

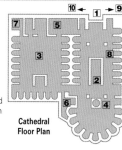

Cathedral Floor Plan

6 Capella de Sant Benet

Honouring Sant Benet, the patron saint of Europe, this chapel showcases the 15th-century altarpiece *Transfiguration of the Lord (below)* by illustrious Catalan artist Bernat Martorell.

7 Capella de Santa Llúcia

This lovely Romanesque chapel is dedicated to Santa Llúcia, the patron saint of sight and vision. On her saint's day (13 December), the blind (*els cecs*) arrive in large numbers to pray at her chapel.

8 Nave & Organ

The immense nave *(below)* is supported by soaring Gothic buttresses, which arch over 16 chapels. The 16th-century organ looming over the interior fills the Cathedral with music during services.

Cathedral Guide

The most impressive entrance to the Cathedral is its main portal on Plaça de la Seu. As you enter, to the left lie a series of chapels, the organ and elevators that take you to the terrace for phenomenal views of the Barri Gòtic (*see p55*). The Casa de L'Ardiaca lies to the right of the Cathedral's main entrance (at Carrer Santa Llúcia 1); the Museu Diocesà is to the left (at Avingunda de la Catedral 4).

9 Pia Almoina & Museu Diocesà

The 11th-century Pia Almoina, once a rest house for pilgrims and the poor, houses the Museu Diocesà, with Romanesque and Gothic works of art from around Catalonia.

10 Casa de L'Ardiaca

Originally built in the 12th century, the Archdeacon's House sits near what was once the Bishop's Gate in the city's Roman walls. Expanded over the centuries, it now includes a leafy patio with a fountain.

For more sights in the Barri Gòtic & La Ribera **See pp70–73**

Parc de la Ciutadella

Unfolding languidly just to the east of the old town, this green, tranquil oasis provides a welcome respite from the city centre. Built in the late 1860s on the site of a former military fortress (ciutadella), the park was artfully designed to offer Barcelona's citizens an experience of nature (shady corners, paths and greenhouses), recreation (rowing boats on the lake) and culture (two museums). The 1888 Universal Exhibition was held here and in preparation

Statuary on the Cascade Fountain

Pick up a picnic at the bustling Santa Caterina food market (northwest of the park), or have a drink and a snack in the pretty outdoor café, El Drac, next to the Castell dels Tres Dragons building.

the city's great Modernista architects were brought in to work their magic. Lluís Domènech i Montaner created the Castell dels Tres Dragons (today part of the Natural Science Museum) and a young Antoni Gaudí helped design the flamboyant Cascade Fountain.

Top 10 Sights

1 Cascade Fountain
2 Arc de Triomf
3 Parc Zoològic
4 Llac
5 Antic Mercat del Born
6 Museu de Ciències Naturals (Castell dels Tres Dragons)
7 Museu de Ciències Naturals (Museu Martorell)
8 Hivernacle & Umbracle
9 Parlament de Catalunya
10 *Homenatge a Picasso*

• Main entrance: Pg Pujades • Map R4
• Park: open 8am–sunset daily; free; • DA
• Zoo: open Nov–Mar: 10am–5:30pm daily; mid-May–mid-Sep: 10am–8pm daily; Apr–mid-May & mid-Sep–Oct: 10am–7pm daily; €19.60, children aged 3–12 €11.80; • DA
• Museu de Ciències Naturals (Museu Martorell): closed for renovation until the end of 2014; €6; • DA

Cascade Fountain

One glimpse of this Baroque-style fountain *(right)* and you'll guess Gaudí had a hand in its creation. Winged horses with serpent tails rear over a waterfall and cherubs play amid jets of water.

Arc de Triomf

The grandest entrance to the park is the Arc de Triomf *(above)*, designed for the 1888 Exhibition by Josep Vilaseca i Casanoves. Topping the arch are angels tooting horns and offering wreaths.

Parc Zoològic

These colourful flamingos are just some of the stars at this child-friendly zoo, which also has pony rides, electric cars and regular dolphin shows *(see p62).*

4 Llac
Located in the centre of the park is a placid, man-made lake *(above)*, where it's possible to rent a boat for half an hour or more.

5 Antic Mercat del Born
The outline of Barcelona's medieval streets, houses, shops and palaces is revealed below this old market, the foundations of which date from 1714. The market now houses a cultural centre.

Park Plan

6 Castell dels Tres Dragons
Domènech i Montaner's striking building is now part of the Natural Science Museum, and houses the library, laboratories and part of the zoological and geological collection. It is open to researchers only.

7 Museu Martorell
Originally a geology museum, this building is now part of the Natural Science Museum. When it reopens, in 2014, it will house an exhibition on the scientific culture of the city.

8 Hivernacle & Umbracle
The late 19th-century Hivernacle and Umbracle greenhouses *(above)* are currently empty pending renovation work. The latter was designed by architect Josep Fontseré, the former by Josep Amargós.

9 Parlament de Catalunya
Housed in the lovely Palau de la Ciutadella *(below)*, 1891, is the Catalonian Parliament, where Artur Mas (the President of Catalonia) and other political groups meet. In front is the Plaça d'Armes and a graceful water-lily pond with a sculpture (1907) by Josep Llimona.

10 Homenatge a Picasso
Antoni Tàpies toasts Picasso's cubist legacy with an abstract creation of his own. Tàpies' *Homage to Picasso* – a large glass cube filled with furnishings and abstract objects – requires some mental gymnastics to decipher its meaning.

Park Guide
Two metro stops provide access to the park: to approach through the grand Arc de Triomf, disembark at the metro station of the same name. If you're heading to the zoo, get off at Barceloneta metro stop, which is within easy walking distance.

⒑ Museu Nacional d'Art de Catalunya

Incorporating one of the most important medieval art collections in the world, the Museu Nacional d'Art de Catalunya (MNAC) is housed in the majestic Palau Nacional, built in 1929. The high point of the museum is the Romanesque art section, consisting of the painted interiors of churches from the Pyrenees dating from the 11th and 12th centuries. There is also the Thyssen-Bornemisza Collection, with works from the Gothic period to the Rococo; the Cambó Bequest, with works by the likes of Goya and Zurbarán; and a collection of works by Catalan artists from the early 19th century to the present day.

Palau Nacional façade

🍽 On the first floor there is an elegant restaurant. There's also a top-notch café in the Oval Room.

🔭 There are great views from the patio by the main entrance and from the roof terrace. There are outdoor cafés there, too.

- Palau Nacional, Parc de Montjuïc • Map B4
- Metro: Espanya; or buses 55 or 150
- 93 622 03 76
- www.mnac.cat
- Open 10am–6pm (8pm Jun–Sep) Tue–Sat, 10am–3pm Sun
- Adm: €12; con €8.40 (valid for two days within one month); free Sat from 3pm and first Sun of the month; free under 16 and over 65 years old; Audioguide €3.20)
- Guided tours by appt and 1st Sun of month (noon in Catalan and 12:15pm in Spanish)
- DA

Top 10 Exhibits

1. Murals: Santa Maria de Taüll
2. Frescoes: Sant Climent de Taüll
3. Crucifix of Batlló Majesty
4. The Madonna of the Councillors
5. Cambó Bequest
6. Thyssen-Bornemisza Collection
7. Ramon Casas and Pere Romeu on a Tandem (1897)
8. Confidant from the Batlló House (1907)
9. Woman with Hat and Fur Collar (1937)
10. Numismatics

First Floor

Key

▨ Romanesque Art Gallery

▨ Modern Art; Drawings, Prints and Posters

▨ Gothic Art Gallery

▨ Renaissance and Baroque Art

▨ Library

1 Murals: Santa Maria de Taüll

The well-preserved interior of Santa Maria de Taüll (c.1123) gives an idea of how incredibly colourful the Romanesque churches must have been. The symbolism concentrates on Jesus's early life, with scenes of the Wise Men and John the Baptist.

2 Frescoes: Sant Climent de Taüll

The Taüll interior *(left)*, is a melange of Byzantine, French and Italian influences. The apse is dominated by *Christ in Majesty* and the symbols of the four Evangelists and the Virgin, with the apostles beneath.

For more sights in Montjuïc See pp88–91

Crucifix of Batlló Majesty

This splendid, mid-12th-century wooden carving *(right)* depicts Christ on the cross with open eyes and no signs of suffering, as he has defeated death.

4 The Madonna of the Councillors

Commissioned by the city council in 1443, this work *(left)* by Lluis Dalmau is rich in political symbolism. It reveals the head councillors, supported by saints and martyrs, kneeling before an enthroned Virgin.

6 Thyssen-Bornemisza Collection
A small but fine selection of Baron Thyssen-Bornemisza's vast collection. Among the magnificent paintings are Fra Angelico's sublime *Madonna of Humility* (1433–5) and a charmingly domestic *Madonna and Child* (c.1618) by Rubens.

5 Cambó Bequest
Catalan politician Francesc Cambó (1876–1974) bequeathed his enormous art collection to Catalunya; two large galleries contain artworks from the 16th to early 19th centuries, including Titian's *Girl Before A Mirror* (c. 1515).

7 Ramon Casas and Pere Romeu on a Tandem
This painting *(above)* depicts the painter Casas and his friend Romeu, with whom he began the bohemian tavern Els Quatre Gats *(see pp44–5)*.

8 Confidant from the Batlló House
Among the fine *Modernista* furnishings are some exquisite pieces by Antoni Gaudí, including this undulating wooden chair *(left)* designed for confidences between friends.

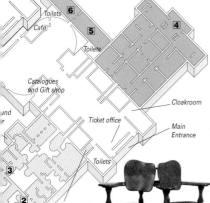

Floorplan labels:
Toilets
Café
Toilets
Catalogues and Gift shop
Cloakroom
Ticket office
Main Entrance
Toilets
Stairs down to temporary exhibitions

9 Woman with Hat and Fur Collar
Picasso's extraordinary depiction of his lover Maria-Thérèse Walter shows him moving beyond Cubism and Surrealism into a new personal language, which would become known simply as the "Picasso style".

10 Numismatics
The public numismatic collection dates back to the 6th century BC and features medals, coins (including those from the Greek colony of Empuries, which had its own mint from the 5th century BC), paper money and 15th-century Italian bills.

Gallery Guide
The Cambó Bequest and the Thyssen-Bornemisza Collections are on the main floor, off the Oval floor. On the first floor are the Modern art galleries, the photography and numismatics collections.

For information on the Font Màgica, located at the bottom of the steps that lead up to the Palau Nacional See p89

TOP 10 La Pedrera

Completed in 1912, this fantastic, undulating apartment block, with its out-of-this-world roof and delicate wrought ironwork, is one of the most emblematic of all Gaudí's works. La Pedrera (the Stone Quarry), also known as Casa Milà, was Gaudí's last great civic work before he dedicated the rest of his life to the Sagrada Família (see pp8–10). Now restored to its former glory, La Pedrera contains the Espai Gaudí, a centre dedicated to the architect, the exhibition hall and offices of the Fundació Catalunya-La Pedrera, and the Pedrera Apartment. What makes La Pedrera so magical is that every detail, from door knobs to light fittings, bears the hallmark of Gaudí's visionary genius.

Façade, La Pedrera

🎵 There are regular classical, jazz and contemporary music concerts held in the auditorium.

For more information on temporary exhibitions held here, check the website of the Catalunya-La Pedrera Foundation (www.lapedrera.com).

- *Pg de Gracia 92*
- *Map E2*
- *902 20 21 38*
- *Metro: Diagonal*
- *Open: El Pis de La Pedrera (furnished apartment) and the Espai Gaudí: 9am–8pm daily (to 6:30pm Nov–Feb); Temporary exhibitions: 10am–8pm daily*
- *Adm: €16.50; con €14.85; Audioguides €4; Advance booking recommended; Free admission to the temporary exhibition space*
- *Night-time guided tours (Nov–Feb: Wed–Sat; Mar–Oct: daily); €30*
- *www.lapedrera.com*

Top 10 Features

1. Façade & Balconies
2. Roof
3. Espai Gaudí
4. El Pis de La Pedrera
5. Interior Courtyard: C/Provença
6. Gates
7. Temporary Exhibition Hall
8. Interior Courtyard: Pg de Gràcia
9. Auditorium
10. La Pedrera Shop & Café

1 Façade & Balconies

Defying the laws of gravity, La Pedrera's irreverent curved walls are held in place by undulating horizontal beams attached to invisible girders. Intricate wrought-iron balconies *(above)* are a perfect example of the artisan skill so integral to *Modernisme*.

3 Espai Gaudí

A series of drawings, photos, maquettes and multimedia displays helps visitors grasp Gaudí's architectural wizardry. The museum is housed in the breathtaking, vaulted attic with its 270 brick arches forming skeletal corridors.

2 Roof

The strikingly surreal rooftop sculpture park *(above)* has chimneys resembling medieval warriors and huge ventilator ducts twisted into bizarre organic forms *(below)*; not to mention good views over the Eixample.

For more on Modernista *architecture* **See pp32–3**

4 El Pis de La Pedrera

This furnished *Modernista* flat *(right)*, decorated with period furniture, is a reconstruction of a typical bourgeois flat of late 19th-century Barcelona. It provides an engaging contrast between the staid middle-class conservatism of the era and the undeniable wackiness of the outer building itself.

5 Interior Courtyard: C/Provença

A brigade of guides takes a multitude of visitors through here each day. A closer inspection of this first courtyard reveals its beautiful mosaics and wall paintings lining a swirling, fairytale staircase.

6 Gates

The mastery involved in these huge, wrought-iron gates reveals the influence of Gaudí's predecessors – four generations of artisan metalworkers. The use of iron is integral to many of Gaudí's buildings.

7 Temporary Exhibition Hall

This gallery space, run by the Catalunya-La Pedrera Foundation, holds regular free art exhibitions. It has shown work by Salvador Dalí, Francis Bacon, Marc Chagall and others. The ceiling *(above)* looks as if it has been coated with whisked egg whites.

8 Interior Courtyard: Pg de Gràcia

Like the first courtyard, here, too, is a grand, ornate staircase (left). This one is adorned with a stunning, floral ceiling painting.

9 Auditorium

The auditorium, located in the former coach-house, hosts regular events such as conferences and concerts. The adjacent garden offers visitors a glimpse of greenery.

10 La Pedrera Shop & Café

A wide range of Gaudí-related memorabilia includes replicas of the warrior chimneys in ceramic and bronze.

Sight Guide

The Espai Gaudí (attic), El Pis (fourth floor) and the rooftop are all accessible by lift. The Temporary Exhibition Hall is located upstairs from the Pg de Gràcia courtyard. The courtyards, staircases and shops are accessible from the entrance on the corner of Pg de Gràcia and C/Provença.

For more on Antoni Gaudí **See p11**

Fundació Joan Miró

This superb tribute to a man whose legacy as an artist and as a Catalan is visible city-wide was founded in 1975 by Joan Miró himself, who wanted it to be a contemporary arts centre. The museum holds more than 14,000 examples of the artist's colourful paintings, sketches and sculptures. The 400 or so on display trace Miró's development from an innovative Surrealist phase in the 1920s to his place as one of the world's most challenging masters in the 1960s.

Façade, Fundació Joan Miró

🍽 The restaurant-café here is one of the best dining options in the area *(see p93)*.

🎵 In summer, live experimental music is showcased in the Fundació auditorium, usually on Thursday nights.

The gift shop has an original range of Miróesque curiosities, from tablecloths to champagne glasses.

• Av Miramar, Parc de Montjuïc
• Map B4
• 93 443 94 70
• www.fundaciomiro-bcn.org
• Metro to Paral·lel, then funicular; or metro to Pl. Espanya, then bus 150; or bus 55 from the city centre
• Open: 10am–7pm Tue, Wed, Fri & Sat (until 8pm Jul–Sep) 10am–9:30pm Thu, 10am–2:30pm Sun
• Adm: €11, con €7; audioguides €5 • DA

Top 10 Works of Art

1. *Tapis de la Fundació* (1979)
2. *L'Estel Matinal* (1940)
3. *Pagès Català al Clar de Lluna* (1968)
4. *Home i Dona Davant un Munt d'Excrement* (1935)
5. *Sèrie Barcelona* (1944)
6. *Font de Mercuri* (1937)
7. Sculpture Room
8. Terrace Garden
9. Visiting Exhibitions
10. Espai 13

Tapis de la Fundació
This immense, richly-coloured tapestry *(right)* represents the culmination of Miró's work with textiles, which began in the 1970s.

L'Estel Matinal
This is one of 23 paintings on paper known as the *Constellation Series*. The *Morning Star's* introspective quality reflects Miró's state of mind at the outbreak of World War II, when he was hiding in Normandy. Spindly shapes of birds, women and heavenly bodies are suspended in an empty space.

Pagès Català al Clar de Lluna
The figurative painting *Catalan Peasant by Moonlight* *(left)* dates from the late 1960s and depicts two of Miró's favourite themes: earth and night. The figure of the peasant, a simple collage of colour, is barely decipherable, as the crescent moon merges with his sickle and the night sky takes on the rich green tones of earth.

Home i Dona Davant un Munt d'Excrement

Tortured, misshapen and lurid semi-abstract figures attempt to embrace against a black sky. Miró's pessimism at the time of *Man and Woman in Front of a Pile of Excrement (right)* would soon be confirmed by the outbreak of Spain's Civil War.

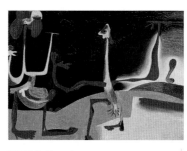

Sèrie Barcelona

The Fundació holds the only complete set of prints of this series of more than 50 black-and-white lithographs. This important collection is only occasionally on display.

Font de Mercuri

Alexander Calder donated the *Mercury Fountain* to the Fundació as a mark of his friendship with Miró. The work was an anti-fascist tribute, conceived in memory of the attack on the town of Almadén.

Sculpture Room

This room *(above)* focuses on Miró's sculptures from the mid-1940s to the late 1950s when he experimented first with ceramic, then bronze and finally with painted media and found objects. Outstanding works include *Sun Bird* (1946–9) and *Moon Bird* (1946–9).

Terrace Garden

More of Miró's vibrantly colourful and playful sculptures are randomly scattered on a spacious terrace *(right)*, from which you can appreciate city views and the rationalist architecture of Josep Lluis Sert's geometric building. The 3-m (10-ft) tall *Caress of a Bird* (1967) dominates the terrace.

Espai 13

This space showcases the experimental work of new artists from around the world. The exhibitions, which are based on a single theme each year, are usually radical and often make full use of new technologies.

Visiting Exhibitions

Over the years, these temporary exhibitions (usually held in the west wing) have included retrospectives of high-profile artists such as Rothko, Warhol and Magritte.

Gallery K. AG

This extension houses 25 paintings on long-term loan from the private collections of members of the Miró family and from Gallery K, founded by Japanese collector Kazumasa Katsuta.

The Fundació's collection is vast; only a portion of it is on show at any one time.

Museu Picasso

Pay homage to the 20th-century's most acclaimed artist at this treasure-filled museum. Highlighting Pablo Picasso's (1881–1973) formative years, the museum boasts the world's largest collection of the artist's early works. At the tender age of 10, Picasso was already revealing remarkable artistic tendencies. In 1895, aged 14, he and his family moved from the town of La Coruña to Barcelona, where Picasso blossomed as an artist. From precocious schoolbook sketches and powerful family portraits to selected works from his Blue and Rose periods, the Museu Picasso offers visitors the rare chance to discover the artist as he was discovering himself.

Entrance, Carrer Montcada

☕ The museum has a café with outdoor tables in summer. It offers a changing menu of daily specials at lunchtimes.

✿ The Museu Picasso is housed in a Gothic palace complex, replete with leafy courtyards, all of which can be explored.

• C/Montcada 15–23
• Map P4 • 93 256 30 00
• www.museupicasso.bcn.cat • Metro: Jaume I
• Open 10am–8pm Tue–Sun • Guided tours: 11am Sun (English), noon Sun (Spanish); (reservations essential, email museupicasso_reserves@bcn.cat)
• Adm: €11; €4.40 (temporary shows); free first Sun of month (permanent collection) and every Sun 3–8pm;
• DA

Top 10 Exhibits

1. *Home amb boina* (1895)
2. *Autoretrat amb perruca* (1896)
3. *Ciència i Caritat* (1897)
4. Menu de Els Quatre Gats (1899–1900)
5. *L'Espera (Margot) & La Nana* (1901)
6. *El Foll* (1904)
7. *Arlequí* (1917)
8. *Cavall banyegat* (1917)
9. *Home assegnt* (1917)
10. *Las Meninas* Series (1957)

Home amb boina

This portrait *(below)* reveals brush strokes – and a subject matter – that are far beyond a 13-year-old child. No puppies or cars for the young Picasso; instead, he painted the portraits of the oldest men in the village. He signed this work P Ruiz, because at this time he was still using his father's last name.

Autoretrat amb perruca

At 14, Picasso painted a series of self-portraits, including *Self-portrait with Wig*, a whimsical depiction of how he might have looked during the time of his artistic hero, Velázquez.

Ciència i Caritat

One of Picasso's first publicly exhibited paintings was *Science and Charity*. Picasso's father posed as the doctor.

4 Menu de Els Quatre Gats

Picasso's premier Barcelona exhibition was in 1900, held at the Barri Gòtic café, Els Quatre Gats *(see p45)*. The artist's first commission was the pen-and-ink drawing of himself and a group of artist friends in top hats, which graced the menu of this bohemian hang-out.

5 L'Espera (Margot) & La Nana

Picasso's *Margot (centre)* is an evocative painting depicting a call-girl as she waits for her next customer, while *La Nana* captures the defiant expression and stance of a heavily rouged female dwarf dancer.

6 El Foll

The Madman (left) is a fine example of Picasso's Blue period. This artistic phase, which lasted from 1901 to 1904, was characterized by melancholic themes and sombre colours.

7 Arlequí

A lifting of spirits led to Picasso's Neo-Classical period, typified by paintings like *Arlequí*, celebrating the light-hearted liberty of circus performers.

8 Cavall banyegat

The anguished horse in this painting later appears in *Guernica*, which reveals the horrors of war. This work gives viewers the chance to observe the process that went into the creation of Picasso's most famous painting.

9 Home assegnt

Works such as *Man Sitting (right)* confirmed Picasso's status as the greatest Analytic Cubist painter of the 20th century.

10 Las Meninas Series

Picasso's reverence for Velázquez culminated in this remarkable series of paintings *(below)*, based on the Velázquez painting *Las Meninas*.

Gallery Guide

The museum is made up of five inter-connected medieval palaces. The permanent collection is arranged chronologically on the first and second floors of the first three palaces. Temporary exhibitions – usually showcasing one modern artist – are housed on the first and second floors of the last two palaces.

10 Palau de la Música Catalana

Barcelona's Modernista movement reached its aesthetic culmination in this magnificent concert hall (1905–8), designed by renowned architect Lluís Domènech i Montaner. The lavish façade, ringed by mosaic pillars and brick arches, just hints at what awaits within. Domènech's "garden of music" (as he called it) unfolds beyond the front doors, with each surface of the ornate foyer, from pillars to banisters, emblazoned with a flower motif. The concert hall – designed so that its height is the same as its breadth – is a celebration of natural light and forms, climaxing in a stained-glass, golden orb skylight that showers the hall with sunlight.

Façade, Palau de la Música Catalana

For a pre-concert, cocktail, settle in at the *Modernista* stained-glass bar just beyond the foyer.

There are concerts for children most Sundays at noon.

Buy tickets for the shows and guided tours from the box office round the corner at C/Palau de la Música 4: (902 442 882), open 9am–9pm daily (from 9:30am Sat & Sun).

- *Sant Pere Més Alt*
- *Map N2*
- *902 47 54 85*
- *www.palaumusica.org*
- *Metro: Urquinaona*
- *Guided tours every 30 mins: Easter & Aug: 10am–8pm; Sep–Jul: 10am–3:30pm (advance booking recommended)*
- *Adm: €17, con €11*
- *Limited DA*

Top 10 Features

1 Stained-Glass Ceiling
2 Stage
3 Stained-Glass Windows
4 Busts
5 Horse Sculptures
6 Rehearsal Hall of the Orfeó Català
7 Lluís Millet Hall
8 Foyer & Bar
9 Façade
10 Concert & Dance Series

1 Stained-Glass Ceiling
Topping the concert hall is a breathtaking, stained-glass inverted dome ceiling *(right)*. By day, light streams through the fiery red and orange stained glass, illuminating the hall.

2 Stage

The main, semicircular stage *(above)* swarms with activity – even when no-one's performing. Eighteen mosaic and terracotta muses spring from the backdrop, playing everything from the harp to the castanets.

3 Stained-Glass Windows
Blurring the boundaries between the outdoors and the interior, Domènech encircled the concert hall with vast stained-glass windows to let in sunlight and reveal the changing times of day.

For more on Modernista architecture **See pp32–3**

4 Busts
A bust of Catalan composer Josep Anselm Clavé (1824–74) celebrates the Palau's commitment to Catalan music. Facing him across the concert hall, a stern-faced, unruly-haired Beethoven *(above)* represents the hall's classical and international repertoire.

5 Horse Sculptures
Charging forth from the ceiling are winged horses (by the sculptor Eusebi Arnau), infusing the concert hall with movement and verve. Also depicted is a representation of Wagner's chariot ride of the Valkyries, led by galloping horses that leap toward the stage.

6 Rehearsal Hall of the Orfeó Català
This semicircular, acoustically-sound rehearsal room is a smaller version of the massive concert hall one floor above. In its centre is an inlaid foundation stone commemorating the construction of the Palau.

7 Lluís Millet Hall
Named after Catalan composer Lluís Millet, this immaculately preserved lounge boasts gorgeous stained-glass windows. On the main balcony outside are rows of stunning mosaic pillars *(right)*.

8 Foyer & Bar
Modernista architects worked with ceramic, stone, wood, marble and glass, all of which Domènech used liberally, most notably in the opulent foyer and bar.

9 Façade
The towering façade *(below)* reveals *Modernista* delights on every level. An elaborate mosaic represents the Orfeó Català choral society, founded in 1891.

10 Concert & Dance Series
Over 500 concerts and dance shows are staged each year, and seeing a show here is a thrilling experience. For symphonic concerts, keep an eye out for the Palau 100 Series; for choral concerts, look out for the Orfeó Català series.

Orfeó Català
Perhaps the most famous choral group to perform here is the Orfeó Català, for whom the concert hall was originally built. This 90-person chorus performs regularly and holds a concert on 26 December every year. Book in advance.

🔟 Museu d'Art Contemporani & Centre de Cultura Contemporània

Barcelona's sleek contemporary art museum looms in bold contrast to the surrounding area. Together with the nearby Centre de Cultura Contemporània (CCCB), the Museu d'Art Contemporani (MACBA) has provided a focal point for modern Barcelona since its opening in 1995, and has played an integral part in the rejuvenation of El Raval. MACBA's permanent collection includes a slew of big-name Spanish and international contemporary artists, while excellent temporary exhibits feature everything from painting to video installations. The

Gallery space, MACBA

🍴 Snack at the nearby restaurant Pla dels Àngels (on Carrer Ferlandina), which offers budget-priced nouvelle/Catalan food to a hip crowd.

- *MACBA*
- *Plaça dels Àngels*
- *Map K2*
- *Metro: Catalunya*
- *93 412 08 10*
- *www.macba.cat*
- *Open Jul–Sep: 11am–8pm Mon, Wed & Thu, 11am–10pm Fri, 10am–10pm Sat, 10am–3pm Sun; late Sep–late Jun: 11am–7:30pm Mon & Wed–Fri, 10am–9pm Sat, 10am–3pm Sun*
- *Adm: €8 (all floors); €6.50 (temporary exhibitions) free for under-14- and over 65-year-olds • DA*

- *CCCB • Montalegre 5*
- *Map K1 • Metro: Catalunya• 93 306 41 00*
- *www.cccb.org*
- *Open: 11am–8pm Tue–Sun*
- *Adm: €5; con €3; free first Wed of month and 3–8pm Sun*

CCCB serves as a crossroads of contemporary culture with cutting-edge art exhibits, lectures and film screenings.

Top 10 Features

1. Interior Corridors
2. Visiting Artist's Space
3. Revolving Permanent Collection
4. Façade
5. Capella MACBA™
6. *A Sudden Awakening*
7. Thinking & Reading Spaces
8. El Pati de les Dones/CCCB
9. Temporary Exhibitions/CCCB
10. Plaça Joan Coromines

1 Interior Corridors
Space and light are omnipresent in the walkways between floors. Look through the glass panels onto the Plaça dels Àngels for myriad images before you even enter the gallery spaces.

2 Visiting Artist's Space
The *raison d'etre* of MACBA is this flexible area showing the best in contemporary art. Past exhibitions have included Zush and acclaimed painter Dieter Roth.

3 Revolving Permanent Collection
The permanent collection comprises over 2000 – mostly European – modern artworks, 10 per cent of which are on show at any one time. All major contemporary artistic trends are represented. This work *(right)* by Eduardo Arranz Bravo is titled *Homea* (1974).

 For more museums **See pp40–41**

Façade
American architect Richard Meier's stark, white, geometrical façade makes a startling impression against the backdrop of this dilapidated working-class neighbourhood. Hundreds of panes of glass reflect the skateboarders who gather here daily.

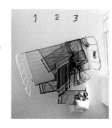

Capella MACBA
One of the few surviving Renaissance chapels in the city has been converted for use as MACBA's temporary exhibition space. It is located in a former convent across the Plaça dels Àngels.

A Sudden Awakening
One of the only pieces of art on permanent display is Antoni Tàpies' deconstructed bed (1992–3), with its bedding flung across the wall in disarray (above). Its presence to the right of the main entrance underlines the late Tàpies' importance in the world of Catalan modern art.

Thinking & Reading Spaces
Pleasant and unusual features of MACBA are the white leather sofas between the galleries. Usually next to a shelf of relevant books and a set of headphones, these spaces provide the perfect resting spot to contemplate – and learn more about – the art.

El Pati de les Dones/CCCB
This courtyard (left) off Carrer Montalegre forms part of the neighbouring CCCB. An ultra-modern prismatic screen provides a mirror reflecting the 18th-century patio – a magical juxtaposition of different architectural styles.

Temporary Exhibitions/CCCB
Unlike MACBA, exhibitions at the CCCB tend to be more theme based than artist specific. Home to both a festival of cinema shorts (Sep) and the Sònar techno festival (Jun), the CCCB always manages to be at the forefront of the latest cultural trend.

Plaça Joan Coromines
The contrast between the modern MACBA, the University building, the Tuscan-style CCCB and the 19th-century mock-Romanesque church make this square one of the most enchanting in the city. It is home to the terrace restaurants of MACBA and CCCB.

Sights Guide
The MACBA and CCCB have separate entrances, though they share the Plaça Joan Coromines courtyard. The CCCB is accessible from C/Montalegre and MACBA from the Plaça dels Àngels. Both multi-level galleries have flexible display spaces.

For more sights in El Raval See pp80–83

Left **La Setmana Tràgica, 1909** Right **Olympic Games, 1992**

Stages in Barcelona's History

1 BC: The Founding of a City
Barcino, as the city was first known, was founded in the 3rd century BC by Carthaginian Hamilcar Barca. It was taken by the Romans in 218 BC, but played second fiddle in the region to the provincial capital of Tarragona.

2 4th–11th Centuries: Early Invasions
As the Roman Empire began to fall apart in the 5th century, the Visigoths took over the city, followed by the Moors in the 8th century. Around AD 800, Charlemagne conquered the area with the help of the Pyrenean counts.

Poster, 1929 International Exhibition

3 12th–16th Centuries: The Middle Ages
During this period, Barcelona was the capital of a Catalan empire that stretched across the Mediterranean. The city's fortune was built on commerce, but as neighbouring Castile expanded into the New World, trading patterns shifted and the Catalan dynasty faltered. Barcelona fell into decline and came under Castilian domination.

4 1638–1652: Catalan Revolt
In reaction to the oppressive policies set out in Madrid, now ruled by the Austrian Habsburgs, various local factions, known as *Els Segadors*, revolted. Fighting began in 1640 and dragged on until 1652, when the Catalans and their French allies were defeated.

5 19th Century: Industry & Prosperity
Booming industry and trade with the Americas brought activity to the city. Immigrants poured in from the countryside, laying the foundations of prosperity but also the seeds of unrest. The old city walls came down, broad Eixample avenues were laid out and workers crowded the old city neighbourhoods left behind by the middle classes.

6 1888–1929: The Renaixença
This new wealth, showcased in the International Exhibitions of 1888 and 1929, sparked a Catalan renaissance. *Modernista* mansions sprouted up, and the nationalist bourgeoisie sparked a revival of Catalan culture.

7 1909–1931: The Revolutionary Years
But discontent brewed among workers, Catalan nationalists, communists, Spanish fascists, royalists, anarchists and republicans. In 1909, protests

against the Moroccan war sparked a brutal riot, the *Setmana Tràgica* (Tragic Week). Lurching towards Civil War, Catalonia passed under a dictatorship before being declared a Republic in 1931.

8 1936–1975: Civil War & Franco
At the outbreak of war in 1936, Barcelona's workers and militants managed to fend off Franco's troops for a while. The city was taken by Fascist forces in 1939, prompting a wave of repression, particularly of the Catalan language which was banned in schools.

9 1975–1980s: Transition to Democracy
Franco's death in 1975 paved the way for democracy. The Catalan language was rehabilitated and Catalonia was granted regional autonomy. The first Catalan government was elected in 1980.

10 1992–Present Day: The Olympics & Beyond
Barcelona was catapulted onto the world stage in 1992 with the highly successful Olympics. In 2011, after 32 years of socialist government, the centre-right Catalan nationalist party (CiU) rose to power in the city. Parties supporting Catalonia independence continue to gain ground.

Civil War, 1936

Top 10 Historical Figures

1 Guifré the Hairy
The first Count of Barcelona (d. 897) is regarded as the founding father of Catalonia.

2 Ramon Berenguer IV
He united Catalonia and joined it with Aragon by marrying Princess Petronila in 1137.

3 Jaume I the Conqueror
This 13th-century warrior-king (d. 1276) conquered the Balearics and Valencia, laying the foundations for the empire.

4 Ramon Llull
Mallorcan philosopher and missionary, Llull (d. 1316) is the greatest figure in medieval Catalan literature.

5 Ferdinand the Catholic
King of Aragon and Catalonia (d.1516), he married Isabel of Castile, paving the way for the Kingdom of Spain's formation and the end of Catalan independence.

6 Idlefons Cerdà
19th-century urban planner who designed the Eixample.

7 Antoni Gaudí
An idiosyncratic and devout *Modernista* architect, Gaudí was responsible for Barcelona's most famous monuments.

8 Francesc Macià
This socialist nationalist politician proclaimed the birth of the Catalan Republic (1931) and Catalan autonomy (1932).

9 Lluís Companys
Catalan president during the Civil War. Exiled in France, he was arrested by the Gestapo in 1940 and returned to Franco, who had him executed.

10 Jordi Pujol
A centre-right regionalist politician, Pujol's Convergència i Unió coalition ruled Catalonia from 1980 to 2003.

Stained-glass windows, Casa Lleò Morera

🔟 Modernista Buildings

1 Sagrada Família
Dizzying spires and intricate sculptures adorn Gaudí's magical masterpiece. Construction began at the height of *Modernisme*, but is still in progress more than a century later. *See pp8–10.*

2 La Pedrera
This amazing apartment block, with its curving façade and bizarre rooftop, has all of Gaudí's architectural trademarks. Especially characteristic are the wrought-iron balconies and the ceramic mosaics decorating the entrance halls. *See pp20–21.*

3 Palau de la Música Catalana
Domènech i Montaner's magnificent concert hall is a joyous celebration of Catalan music. Ablaze with mosaic friezes, stained glass, ceramics and sculptures, it displays the full glory of the *Modernista* style. The work of Miquel Blay on the façade is rated as one of the best examples of *Modernista* sculpture in Barcelona. *See pp26–7.*

4 Hospital de la Santa Creu i de Sant Pau
In defiant contrast to the Eixample's symmetrical grid-like pattern, this ambitious project was planned around two avenues running at 45-degree angles to the Eixample streets. Started by Domènech i Montaner in 1905 and later completed by his son in 1930, the hospital pavilions are lavishly embellished with mosaics, stained glass and sculptures by Eusebi Arnau. The octagonal columns with floral capitals are inspired by those in the Monestir de Santes Creus *(see p124)*, to the south of Barcelona. *See p103.*

5 Fundaciò Tàpies
With a rationally plain façade alleviated only by its *Mudéjar*-style brick work, this austere building, dating to 1886, was originally home to the publishing house Montaner i Simón. It bears the distinction of being the first *Modernista* work to be designed by Domènech i Montaner, which explains why it has so few of the ornate decorative touches that distinguish his later works. Home to the Fundaciò Tàpies, it is now dominated by an enormous sculpture by the contemporary Catalan artist, Antoni Tàpies. *See p104.*

Chimneys and rooftop, Casa Batlló

A ticket for La Ruta Modernista *includes discounted entry to many* Modernista *buildings and a map/guide* See p133

Casa Batlló

6 Illustrating Gaudí's nationalist sentiments, Casa Batlló, on La Mansana de la Discòrdia *(see p103)*, is an allegory of the legend of Sant Jordi *(see p39)*. The roof is the dragon's back, and the balconies, sculpted in the form of carnival masks, are the skulls of the dragon's victims. The façade reveals Gaudí's remarkable use of colour and texture.
🔷 *Pg de Gràcia 43 • Map E2 • Open 9am–8pm daily • 93 216 03 06 • www.casabatllo.es • Adm €20.35 (audioguide included) • DA*

Casa de les Punxes

Casa Amatller

7 The top of Casa Amatller's façade bursts into a brilliant display of blue, cream and pink ceramics with burgundy florets. Architect Puig i Cadafalch's exaggerated decorative use of ceramics is typical of *Modernisme*. Tours include the *Modernista* apartment, a slide show in Amatller's former photography studio and describe the neo-medieval vestibule.
🔷 *Pg de Gràcia 41 • Map E2 • Museum: call ahead for opening hours; tours by appt • 93 496 12 45 • www.amatller.org • Adm €10 • DA*

Palau Güell

8 This is a fine example of Gaudí's experiments with structure, especially the use of parabolic arches to orchestrate space. He also used unusual building materials, such as ebony and rare South American woods. *See p81.*

Casa de les Punxes (Casa Terrades)

9 Taking *Modernisme's* Gothic and medieval obsessions to extremes that others seldom dared, Puig i Cadafalch created this imposing, castle-like structure between 1903 and 1905. Nicknamed the "House of Spines" because of its sharp, needle-like spires rising up from conical turrets, its true name is Casa Terrades. The flamboyant spires contrast with a façade that is, by *Modernista* standards, sparsely decorated.
🔷 *Diagonal 416 • Map F2 • Closed to public*

Casa Lleó Morera

10 Ironwork, ceramics, sculpture and stained glass come together here in a synthesis of the decorative and fine arts. The interior of this house, by Domènech i Montaner, has some superb sculptures by Eusebi Arnau and some of the finest *Modernista* furniture in existence. 🔷 *Pg de Gràcia 35 • Map E3 • Closed to public*

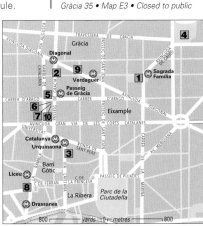

Left **Plaça de Catalunya** Right **Plaça Reial, Barri Gòtic**

🔟 Perfect Squares

Plaça Reial
The arcaded Plaça Reial, in the heart of the Barri Gòtic, is unique among Barcelona's squares, with its old-world charm, gritty urbanization and Neo-Classical flair. It is home to majestic, mid-19th-century buildings, Gaudí lampposts, a slew of happening bars and clubs, and an entertaining and colourful crowd of inner-city denizens. *See p72.*

Plaça de Catalunya
Barcelona's nerve centre is the huge Plaça de Catalunya, a lively hub from which all the city's activity seems to radiate. This square is most visitors' first real glimpse of Barcelona. The airport bus stops here, as do RENFE trains and countless metro and bus lines as well as most night buses. The square's commercial swagger is evident all around, headed by Spain's omnipresent department store, El Corte Inglés *(see p139)*. Pigeons flutter chaotically in the square's centre, lively Peruvian bands play to booming sound systems and hordes of travellers – from backpackers to tour groups – meander about. The main tourist information office is here too. ✪ *Map M1*

Plaça del Rei
One of the city's best pre-served medieval squares, the Barri Gòtic's Plaça del Rei is ringed by grand buildings. Among them is the 14th-century Palau Reial *(see p71)*, which houses the Saló del Tinell, a spacious Catalan Gothic throne room and banqueting hall. ✪ *Map N4*

Plaça de Sant Jaume
Weighty with power and history, this is the administrative heart of modern-day Barcelona. The *plaça* is flanked by the city's two key government buildings, the stately Palau de la Generalitat and the 15th-century Ajuntament. *See p71.*

Café, Plaça Sant Josep Oriol, Barri Gòtic

5 Plaça de la Vila de Gràcia

The progressive, bohemian area of Gràcia, a former village annexed by Barcelona in 1897, still exudes a small-town ambience, where socializing with the neighbours means heading for the nearest *plaça*. Topping the list is this atmospheric square, with an impressive clock tower rising out of its centre. Bustling outdoor cafés draw buskers and a sociable crowd. ✎ *Map F1*

Façade, Plaça del Pi

6 Plaça de Sant Josep Oriol & Plaça del Pi

Old-world charm meets café culture in the Barri Gòtic's leafy Plaça de Sant Josep Oriol and Plaça del Pi, named after the pine trees (*pi*, in Catalan) that shade its nooks and crannies. The lovely Gothic church of Santa Maria del Pi *(see p38)* rises between the two squares. ✎ *Map M3 & M4*

7 Plaça Comercial

The buzzy Passeig del Born culminates in Plaça Comercial, an inviting square dotted with cafés and bars. It faces the 19th-century Born Market *(see p72)*, which has been transformed into a cultural centre and exhibition space. ✎ *Map P4*

8 Plaça del Sol

Tucked within the cosy grid of Gràcia, this square is surrounded by handsome 19th-century buildings. As evening descends, it becomes one of the most lively spots to start your night-time festivities, along with all the *Barcelonins* who mingle on the outdoor terraces. ✎ *Map F1*

9 Plaça de Santa Maria

The magnificent Església de Santa Maria del Mar *(see p76)* imbues its namesake *plaça*, in the El Born district, with a certain spiritual calm. Bask in its Gothic ambience, people watch, and soak up the sun at one of the outdoor terrace cafés. ✎ *Map N5*

10 Plaça de la Vila de Madrid

Mere steps from La Rambla *(see pp12–13)* is this spacious *plaça*, graced with the remains of a Roman necropolis. A remnant of Roman Barcino, the square sat just beyond the boundaries of the walled Roman city. A row of unadorned 2nd–4th-century AD tombs were discovered here in 1957. The complete remains are open to the public. ✎ *Map M2*

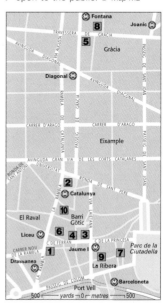

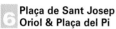

Left **Església del Betlem** Right **Temple Expiatori del Sagrat Cor**

Charming Churches & Chapels

1 Barcelona Cathedral

Barcelona's magnificent Gothic cathedral boasts an eye-catching façade and a peaceful cloister. *See pp14–15.*

2 Església de Santa Maria del Mar

The elegant church of Santa Maria del Mar (1329–83) is one of the finest examples of Catalan Gothic, a style characterized by measured simplicity. A spectacular stained-glass rose window illuminates the lofty interior. *See p76.*

3 Capella de Sant Miquel & Església al Monestir de Pedralbes

Inside the Monestir de Pedralbes *(see p111)* is a Gothic cloister and the Capella de Sant Miquel, decorated with murals by Catalan artist Ferrer Bassa in 1346. The adjoining Gothic church contains the alabaster tomb of Queen Elisenda, the monastery's founder.
🅢 C/Baixada del Monestir 14 • Map A1
• Open Apr–Sep: 10am–5pm Tue–Fri, 10am–7pm Sat, 10am–8pm Sun (church also open 7–8:30pm); Oct–Mar: 10am–2pm Tue–Fri, 10am–5pm Sat & Sun • Adm

4 Església de Sant Pau del Camp

Founded as a Benedictine monastery in the 9th century by Guifre II, a count of Barcelona, this church was rebuilt the following century. Its sculpted façade

and intimate cloister with rounded arches bear all the trademarks of the Romanesque style. *See p83.*

5 Església de Sant Pere de les Puelles

Santa Eulàlia, Barcelona Cathedral

Built in 801 as a chapel for troops stationed in Barcelona, this *església* later became a spiritual retreat for young noble women. The church was rebuilt in the 1100s and is notable today for its Romanesque central cupola and a series of capitals topped with carved leaves. Look out for two stone tablets depicting a Greek cross, which are from the original chapel.
🅢 Pl de Sant Pere • Map P2
• Open 8:30am–1pm, 5–7:30pm Mon–Fri; 8:30am–1pm, 4:30–7pm Sat; 11am–2pm Sun

6 Església de Santa Maria del Pi

This lovely Gothic church with its ornate stained-glass windows graces Plaça del Pi *(see p37).*
🅢 Pl del Pi • Map L3 • Open 9:30am–1pm, 5–8:30pm daily • DA

7 Capella de Santa Àgata

Within the Palau Reial *(see p71)* is the medieval Capella de Santa Àgata, with its 15th-century altarpiece. The chapel can only be visited as part of the Museu d'Història de Barcelona *(see p40).* 🅢 Pl del Rei • Map N3
• Open 10am–7pm Tue–Sat, 10am–8pm Sun • Adm (free 3–8pm Sun)

8 Temple Expiatori del Sagrat Cor

Mount Tibidabo is an appropriate perch for this huge, over-the-top Neo-Gothic church, topped with a gold Christ with outstretched arms. The name Tibidabo takes its meaning from the words, "I shall give you" (*tibi dabo*), uttered by the Devil in his temptation of Christ. Zealously serving the devoted, the priest here performs the Eucharist throughout the day. ✪ *Tibidabo • Map B1 • Open 10:30am–7:30pm daily*

9 Capella de Sant Jordi

Inside the Palau de la Generalitat (*see p71*) is this fine 15th-century chapel, dedicated to Catalonia's patron saint. ✪ *Pl Sant Jaume • Map M4 • Guided tours 10:30am–1:30pm 2nd & 4th Sat & Sun of month; reservations essential*

10 Església de Betlem

La Rambla was once dotted with religious buildings, most built in the 17th and 18th centuries, when the Catholic Church was flush with money. This *església* is one of the major functioning churches from this period. ✪ *C/Xuclà 2 • Map L3 • Open 8:30am–1:30pm & 6–9pm daily • DA*

Gothic nave, Capella de Santa Àgata

Top 10 Catalan Saints & Virgins

1 Sant Jordi
Catalonia's patron saint is Saint George, whose dragon-slaying prowess is depicted all over the city.

2 Virgin Mercè
She became the female patron saint of Barcelona in 1637. The most raucous festival in town is the Festes de La Mercè (*see p64*).

3 Virgin of Montserrat
Catalonia's famous "Black Virgin" is the city's patron virgin.

4 Santa Eulàlia
Santa Eulàlia, Barcelona's first female patron saint, was martyred by the Romans when they took the city.

5 Santa Elena
Legend has it that Saint Helena converted to Christianity after discovering Christ's cross in Jerusalem in 346 AD.

6 Santa Llúcia
The saint of eyes and vision is celebrated on 13 December, when the blind come to worship at the Santa Llúcia chapel in the cathedral (*see pp14–15*).

7 Sant Cristòfol
Though officially stripped of his sainthood as there was little evidence he existed, Saint Christopher was once the patron saint of travellers.

8 Sant Antoni de Padua
On 13 June, those seeking a husband or wife pray to the patron saint of love.

9 Santa Rita
Deliverer of the impossible, Santa Rita is prayed to by those searching for miracles.

10 Sant Joan
The night of Saint John (*see p64*) is celebrated with giant bonfires and fireworks.

Left **Frank Gehry's *Peix*** *Right* **Camp Nou Stadium**

🔟 Museums

1 Museu Nacional d'Art de Catalunya

Discover Catalonia's Romanesque and Gothic heritage at this impressive museum, housed in the 1929 Palau Nacional. Striking medieval frescoes and a collection of *Modernista* furnishings and artworks are highlights. *See pp18–19.*

2 Fundació Joan Miró

The airy, high-ceilinged galleries of this splendid museum are a fitting resting place for the bold, abstract works of Joan Miró, one of Catalonia's most acclaimed 20th-century artists. *See pp22–3.*

3 Museu Picasso

Witness the budding – and meteoric rise – of Picasso's artistic genius at this unique museum. One of the world's largest collections of the painter's early works. *See pp24–5.*

4 Museu d'Art Contemporani & Centre de Cultura Contemporània

Inaugurated in 1995, MACBA is Barcelona's centre for modern art. Combined with the neighbouring CCCB, the two buildings form an artistic and cultural hub in the heart of El Raval. Both regularly host temporary exhibitions: the MACBA showcases contemporary artists; the CCCB is more theme-based. *See pp28–9.*

5 Fundació Tàpies

Works by Catalan artist Antoni Tàpies are showcased in this graceful *Modernista* building. Venture inside to discover Tàpies' rich repertoire, from early collage works to large, abstract paintings, many alluding to political and social themes. *See p104.*

Terrace, Fundació Tàpies

6 Museu d'Història de Barcelona (MUHBA)

Explore the medieval Palau Reial and wander among the splendid remains of Barcelona's Roman walls and waterways at the city's history museum. The museum is partly housed in the 15th-century Casa Padellàs on the impressive medieval Plaça del Rei. *See p71.*

Badge, FC Barcelona

7 Museu del FC Barcelona

This shrine to the city's football club draws a mind-boggling number of fans paying homage to their team. Trophies, posters and other memorabilia celebrate the club's 100-year history. Also visit the adjacent Camp Nou Stadium. *See p111.*

Museu Marítim

Barcelona's formidable sea-faring history is showcased in the cavernous, 13th-century Drassanes Reials (Royal Ship-yards). The collection, which spans from the Middle Ages to the 19th century, includes a full-scale replica of the *Real*, the flagship galley of Don Juan of Austria, who led the Christians to victory against the Turks during the Battle of Lepanto in 1571. Also on display are model ships, maps and navigational instruments. *See p81.*

Museu Frederic Marès

Catalan sculptor Frederic Marès (1893–1991) was a passionate and eclectic collector. Housed here, under one roof,

are many remarkable finds amassed during his travels. Among the vast array of historical objects on display are Romanesque and Gothic religious art and sculptures, plus everything from dolls and fans to pipes and walking sticks. *See p72.*

Virgin, Museu Frederic Marès

CosmoCaixa Museu de la Ciència

Exhibits covering the whole history of science, from the Big Bang to the computer age, are housed in this modern museum. Highlights include an interactive tour of the geological history of our planet, an area of real Amazonian rain forest, and a planetarium. There are also temporary displays on environmental issues and activities for all the family. *See p112.*

Top 10 Quirky Museums/Monuments

1 Museu d'Idees i Invents
An unique museum of ideas and inventions to stimulate creativity. ✆ *C/Ciutat 7 • Map E4*

2 Centre d'Interpretació del Call
Artifacts from Barcelona's medieval Jewish community. ✆ *Pl de Manuel Ribé • Map M4*

3 Museu de la Màgia
A museum devoted to magic, with a collection dating from the 18th century. ✆ *Carrer Jonqueres 15 • Map N2*

4 Museu dels Autòmates
A colourful museum of human and animal automatons. ✆ *Parc d'Atraccions del Tibidabo • Map B1*

5 Museu de la Xocolata
A celebration of chocolate, with interactive exhibits, edible city models and tastings. ✆ *Carrer Comerç 36 • Map P4*

6 Museu de Cera
Over 350 wax figures, from Marilyn Monroe to Franco and Gaudí. ✆ *Ptge de la Banca 7 • Map L5*

7 Museu del Calçat
Footwear from all ages, including shoes worn by famous folks. ✆ *Pl de Sant Felip Neri 5 • Map M3*

8 Museu del Perfum
Hundreds of perfume bottles from Roman times to the present. ✆ *Pg de Gràcia 39 • Map E2*

9 Cap de Barcelona
Pop artist Roy Lichtenstein's "Barcelona Head" (1992). ✆ *Pg de Colom • Map N5*

10 Peix
Frank Gehry's huge shimmering fish sculpture (1992). ✆ *Port Olímpic • Map G5*

Left **Café de l'Òpera, La Rambla** Right **Waterside dining, Port Vell**

Cafés & Light Bites

Café Bliss

1 Hidden down a tiny side street, in one of the loveliest Gothic squares in the old city, is this delightful café. There is a bright terrace, comfy sofas and a range of international magazines and newspapers to browse through. It is perfect for coffee, cakes, light meals or a romantic drink in the evening. *See p78.*

Café de l'Òpera

2 Kick back at this elegant, late 19th-century café while being tended to by vested *cambrers* (waiters). This former *xocolateria* (confectionary café) – named after the Liceu opera house opposite – still serves fine gooey delights such as *xurros amb xocolata* (strips of fried dough with thick chocolate). It's perfect for people-watching on La Rambla. ◈ *La Rambla 74 • Map L4*

Drac Café

3 This tiny outdoor café is located next to the Castell dels Tres Dracs (now part of the Natural History Museum). It has cushioned wicker chairs, huge fans and a menu of fresh sandwiches, tapas and light meals. ◈ *Parc de la Ciutadella • Map Q4 • Closed Dec–Feb*

Bar Lobo

4 This chic café is a popular brunch spot during the day, but it really comes alive in the evenings. From Thursday to Saturday, the second floor becomes a hip club, with guest DJs and a chill-out space. ◈ *Pintor Fortuny, 3 • Map Q4 • 93 481 53 46 • Closed Sun eve and for occasional events • DA*

Federal Café

5 The airy Federal Café is a local hipster hangout serving amazing coffee, brunch and light meals, as well as cocktails in the evening. There is a romantic little roof terrace, free Wi-Fi and English-language magazines to flick through. ◈ *C/Parlament 39 • Map D4 • 93 187 36 07 • Closed Mon*

Bar Kasparo

6 This laid-back, outdoor café serves a sprightly menu of fresh, international fare with an Asiatic twist, including chicken curry and Greek salad. After the sun dips beneath the horizon, a bar-like vibe takes over, fuelled by beer and cider. ◈ *Pl Vicenç Martorell 4 • Map L2 • Closed Jan*

Bar Lobo

All food and drink names are given in Catalan, but in many cases the Castilian variant is used just as commonly.

7 Mandarrosso Pastis

Near the Santa Caterina market, this small café furnished with antiques offers home-made Italian desserts, such as *sfogliatelli* (shell-shaped pastries) and *cannoli*.

◈ C/General Alvarez de Castro 5–7 • Map N3 • 93 319 05 02 • Closed Mon

El Jardí

8 Laie Llibreria Cafè

Tuck into a generous buffet of rice, pasta, greens, chicken and more at this charming, long-running Eixample café-bookshop. You can also opt for the well-priced vegetarian menu, including soup, salad and a main dish. *See p108.*

9 Granja Dulcinea

The *xocolateries* and *granjes* along Carrer Petritxol (see p74) have been satiating sugar cravings for decades. Among them is this old-fashioned café with to-die-for delights, from *xurros amb xocolata* to strawberries and whipped cream. In the summer, delicious *orxates* and *granissats* are on the menu.

◈ C/Petritxol 2 • Map L3 • Closes at 9pm

10 El Jardí

This outdoor café-bar occupies a corner of the Gothic courtyard in front of the medieval hospital of Santa Creu. It is a great spot for a quiet drink, and there is live jazz in the summer. During the winter gas heaters are brought outside. *See p87.*

Top 10 Café Drinks

1 Cafè amb llet
Traditionally enjoyed in the morning, *cafè amb llet* is an ample cup of milky coffee.

2 Tallat & Cafè Sol
Need a fortifying caffeine fix? Try a *tallat*, a small cup of coffee with a dash of milk. A *cafè sol* is just plain coffee. In the summer, opt for either one *amb gel* (with ice).

3 Cigaló
For coffee with a bite, try a *cigaló (carajillo)*, which has a shot of alcohol, usually *conyac* (cognac), *whisky* or *ron* (rum).

4 Orxata
This sweet, milky-white drink made from a tuber (tiger nut) is a summertime favourite.

5 Granissat
Slake your thirst with a cool *granissat*, a crushed-ice drink, usually lemon flavoured.

6 Aigua
Stay hydrated with *aigua mineral* (mineral water) – *amb gas* is sparkling, *sense gas*, still.

7 Cacaolat
Chocolate lovers swoon over this chocolate-milk concoction, one of Spain's most popular sweet drink exports.

8 Una Canya & Una Clara
Una canya is roughly a quarter of a litre of *cervesa de barril* (draft beer). *Una clara* is the same, but with fizzy lemonade mixed in.

9 Cava
Catalonia's answer to champagne is its home-grown *cava*, of which Freixenet and Codorníu are the most famous brands.

10 Sangría
This ever-popular concoction of red wine, fruit juices, and liquors is ordered at cafés throughout the city.

Left **Cinc Sentits** Right **Comerç 24**

Best Restaurants & Tapas Bars

1 La Taverna del Clínic
Slightly off the beaten track, this ordinary-looking tavern offers inventive (if pricey) tapas accompanied by a great array of wines. Arrive early or be prepared to wait. *See p109.*

Wall tile advertising Barcelona restaurant

2 Igueldo
Basque cuisine, prepared with flair and originality, is served in elegant surroundings. Dishes include pig's trotters stuffed with *morcilla* (black pudding) and dried peach purée, or *zamburiñas*, a small scallop from the Atlantic. There is also a tapas bar at the entrance. *See p109.*

3 El Asador d'Aranda
This palatial restaurant, perched high above the city on Tibidabo, dishes up the best in Castilian cuisine. Sizeable starters include *pica pica*, a tasty array of sausages, peppers and hams. The signature main dish is *lechazo* (young lamb) roasted in a wood-fired oven. *See p117.*

Paella

4 Kaiku
This unassuming, beachfront restaurant makes possibly the best paella in the city. It is on the menu as *arròs del xef*, and is prepared with smoked rice and succulent shellfish. The desserts are great too. In the summer book a table on the terrace and enjoy the views and sea breeze. *See p101.*

5 Windsor
The modern Catalan *haute cuisine* dishes served here are based on seasonal local produce. Tasting menus feature *suquet de rape* (monkfish stew) and suckling lamb. *See p109.*

6 Alkimia
The minimalist decor here ensures that the focus is firmly on the food. Chef Jordi Vilà has won countless awards for his innovative Catalan cuisine. Diners can enjoy a tasting menu for €88 and there is also a good set lunch for €39. *C/Indústria 79 • Map G1 • 93 207 61 15 • Closed Sat & Sun, Easter, 3 weeks in Aug • €€€€€*

7 Cinc Sentits
This elegant restaurant is known for its innovative cuisine. The tasting menu, created by chef Jordi Artal, can be paired with specially chosen wines. The set-price lunch menu, available from Monday to Friday, is a bargain. *See p109.*

All food and drink names are given in Catalan, but in many cases the Castilian variant is used just as commonly.

Pez Vela

8 The contemporary decor and fresh Mediterranean cuisine, coupled with some of the best sea views in the city, make this an ideal spot for a special meal. Pez Vela is located underneath the W Hotel. ⊗ *Passeig del Mare Nostrum 19/21 • 93 221 63 17 • Closed Sun dinner • €€€€*

Tickets Bar

9 This restaurant serves tapas with a difference. The exciting menu boasts dishes such as hedgehog with avocado and mint jelly, for example, or Manchego cheese ice cream with bacon, mustard sauce and crunchy cucumber. Book online. A corridor leads to the adjacent cocktail bar, 41°. ⊗ *Avingura Paral.lel 164 • Map C4 • Closed Tue–Fri lunch, Sun, Mon, Easter, 2 weeks in Aug • DA • €€€€*

Igueldo

Comerç 24

10 Perhaps one of the most adventurous restaurants in the city, Comerç 24 has an innovative head chef, Carles Abellan. The constantly changing menu consists of a series of *platillos* (small dishes), which fuse an extraordinary variety of flavours and textures. Try the quail lollipops, sea urchins with foie gras ice cream, or gold-wrapped macadamia nuts. *See p79.*

Top 10 Tapas

1 **Patates Braves**
This traditional tapas favourite consists of fried potatoes topped with a spicy sauce. Equally tasty are *patates* heaped with *alioli* (garlic mayonnaise).

2 **Calamars**
A savoury seafood option is *calamars* (squid) *a la romana* (deep-fried in batter) or *a la planxa* (grilled).

3 **Pa amb Tomàquet**
A key part of any tapas spread is this bread topped with tomato and olive oil.

4 **Croquetes**
A perennial favourite are croquettes; tasty fried morsels of bechamel, usually with ham, chicken or cod.

5 **Musclos o Escopinyes**
Sample Barcelona's fruits of the sea with tapas of tasty mussels or cockles.

6 **Truita de Patates**
The most common tapas dish is this thick potato omelette, often topped with *alioli*.

7 **Ensaladilla Russa**
This "Russian salad" includes potatoes, onions, tuna (and often peas, carrots and other vegetables), all generously enveloped in mayonnaise.

8 **Gambes al'allet**
An appetizing dish of fried prawns (shrimp) coated in garlic and olive oil.

9 **Pernil Serrà**
Cured ham is a Spanish obsession. The best, and most expensive, is Extremadura's speciality, Jabugo.

10 **Fuet**
Embotits (Catalan sausages) include the ever-popular *fuet*, a dry, flavourful variety, most famously produced in the Catalonian town of Vic.

Elephant

⟦TOP 10⟧ Night-time Hot Spots

1 Elephant

Housed in a *Modernista* villa, filled with candles and Moroccan lamps, this swish nightclub attracts a fashionable young crowd. But the real highlight is the garden, where lounge beds with diaphanous white drapes, fountains and giant elephant statues add an exotic touch. In winter, the outdoor dance floor is transformed into a spectacular tent. See p116.

Decoration, Elephant Club

2 Marsella

Founded in 1820, this atmospheric throwback, run by the fifth generation of the Lamiel family, sits in the heart of the Barri Xinès *(see p82)*. Marsella is one of the few places in town where you can enjoy the potent drink absinthe (*absenta*). Settle in at one of the wrought-iron *Modernista* tables, surrounded by ancient mirrors and old religious statues, and test your mettle with the potent yellow liquor that is specially bottled for the bar. See p86.

Sala BeCool

3 Otto Zutz

A swanky Barcelona night-life institution, this three-storey disco is on the itinerary for well-heeled media types. The music verges on the main-stream, with big-name DJs spinning everything from techno to contemporary favourites. See p116.

4 Sala Apolo

A converted theatre, now home to one of the city's best live music and club venues. The Nasty Mondays and Nitsa club nights are veritable institutions. Check the website for up-to-date programme information. See p67.

5 Macarena Club

This minuscule but hugely popular club is located down a narrow street off the Plaça Reial. It features the best local and international DJs playing the latest dance and electronica.
- Ⓢ *C/Nou de Sant Francesc 5 • Map L5*
- *Open from midnight every night*
- *www.macarenaclub.com*

6 La Terrrazza

Located inside the Poble Espanyol *(see p91)*, La Terrrazza is one of the most popular summer nightclubs in Barcelona. The patio becomes the dance-floor, the porches are bars and the garden provides a refreshing chill-out area. Ⓢ *Poble Espanyol, Av Marquès de Comillas • Map A3*
- *Open Thu–Sun (May–Sep) • Adm*

7 Sala BeCool

This stylish club has become a staple on Barcelona's busy party scene. Situated in the chic, uptown Sant Gervasi neighbourhood, the multi-functional space has everything from live music, to club nights and theme parties. Downstairs there are hugely popular DJ sessions offering electro, techno and minimal music from Friday to Saturday; upstairs plays the latest indie hits. The website has a complete listing of the full weekly programme. *See p116.*

Inside Razzmatazz

8 Milano

Be careful not to miss it: stairs that are hidden from the street take you down to an elegant world of red velvet sofas, occasional live jazz and barmen who are experts in making cocktails. Rather than a crowded and noisy atmosphere, this is a den for good conversation, and it's a popular gathering place for writers and journalists. A menu of aperitifs, snacks and drinks should please all tastes, but make sure you sample a Bloody Mary. *See p107.*

9 Jamboree

Venture underground – quite literally – to this popular, hopping jazz club-cum-nightclub in a vaulted space beneath Plaça Reial. Nightly live jazz sessions kick off around 11pm. DJs take over later with dance-inducing sounds. *See p77.*

Jamboree

10 Razzmatazz

This is nothing less than the city's best all-round nightlife venue. Music bands from around the world have played at Razzmatazz, and concerts have included Antony and the Johnsons, the Arctic Monkeys and Róisín Murphy. On Friday and Saturday nights (1am–6am), the venue is divided into five clubs, each with its own distinct individual theme. The club regularly hosts international guest DJs, including big names such as Jarvis Cocker, Shaun Rider and Peter Smith among others. *See p100.*

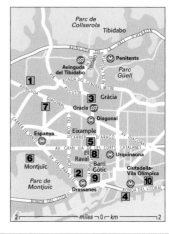

Left **Club scene, Sitges** Right **Punto BCN**

Gay & Lesbian Hang-outs

1 Antinous Llibreria-Cafè
Antinous is a popular, gay meeting point just off the southern end of La Rambla. The café incorporates a spacious shop, stocking gifts, books and videos, and has a small bar area with exhibitions. Pick up a copy of *Nois*, a free magazine available in most gay venues, which gives the lowdown on the gay scene.
🏛 *C/Josep Anselm Clavé 6 • Map L6 • Closed Sun • DA*

Party-goers at a club

2 Dietrich Gay Teatro Café
A gay venue with a mixed door policy, Dietrich is a trendy club with attractive golden walls and an internal garden. As well as playing house and garage music, it features performances by drag artists, dancers and acrobats. 🏛 *Consell de Cent 255 • Map D3*

3 El Cangrejo
A historical venue, this kitsch and lively bar in the Raval is renowned for its 80s nights and drag shows (from 11:30pm at weekends). Dance sessions last until 3am. 🏛 *C/Montserrat 9 • Map K5 • Closed Sun–Wed • DA*

4 Sauna Casanova
This gay sauna (for men only) is ultra-clean, and includes Turkish baths, jacuzzis and saunas, as well as a handy bar and Internet service. There are also private cabins, some with TV screens and DVDs.
🏛 *C/Casanova 57 • Map D3 • Adm*

5 Bim Bam Bum
One of the hottest club-bars in town, Bim Bam Bum has trendy decor, in the style of a loft apartment, and really pulls in the crowds. A heady mix of testosterone, potent drinks and pumping house makes this a prime spot to mingle with some of Barcelona's beauties. 🏛 *C/Casanova 71 • Map D3 • Closed Mon & Tue*

6 Arena Madre
A popular gay disco with a vibrant atmosphere and live performances ranging from

Books, Antinous Llibreria-Cafè

Visit the website www.visitbarcelonagay.com for more information on gay-friendly restaurants, bars and shops.

cheeky strip-teases to drag
shows. The dance floor gets
packed with a fun-loving crowd
enjoying electronic and house
music. There is also a dark room.
🅢 Carrer Balmes 32 • Map E3 • Open
midnight–5am daily • Adm • DA

Metro
The men-only Metro has two
dance floors, one playing house,
while the other has a free-and-
easy music policy and a pool
table. The club only livens up
around 2am. You can sometimes
pick up free tickets at nearby
Dietrich restaurant, another gay
haunt. 🅢 C/Sepúlveda 185 • Map J1
• Adm • DA

Museum
A Luis XV Rococo-style
interior evokes the atmosphere of
a museum, with replicas of
Michelangelo's David on display.
It opens from 10pm for quiet
drinks and turns into a club later
on. The music is commercial pop,
and it gets very busy at weekends. 🅢 Sepúlveda 178 • Map D3
• Closed Sun • DA

Punto BCN
This relaxed, friendly bar has
stayed in vogue for many years
on a fickle gay scene. It gets
impossibly busy around midnight
at weekends and the music is
loud, but it's a good place to get
fired up for a night out and get
the latest on what else is happening in town. 🅢 C/Muntaner 63
• Map D3 • DA

Beaches
In summer, gay men gather
for some sun, fun and plenty of
posing in front of the Club
de Natació Barcelona on
Barceloneta beach near Plaça del
Mar; the Mar Bella beach is also
popular. 🅢 Map E6

Top 10 Gay Hot Spots in Sitges

XXL
Popular with the in-crowd,
with nice decor, a good drinks
selection and techno music.
🅢 C/Joan Tarrida 7

Parrots
A classic Sitges meeting
point, this bar has drag queen
waiters and a lovely outdoor
terrace. 🅢 Plaça Indústria 2

El Mediterráneo
This multi-space bar with
its original design is open in
summer only.
🅢 C/St Bonaventura 6

Trailer
Sitges' oldest gay disco is
always packed with friendly
faces. 🅢 C/Àngel Vidal 36 • Adm

Organic
Organic is a hot disco on
the gay scene, frequented by
a fashion-industry crowd.
🅢 C/Bonaire 15 • Adm

Beaches
The beach in front of the
Hotel Calípolis in Sitges' centre
is a gay magnet, as is the
nudist one on the way to the
town of Vilanova.

Night-time Cruising
The pier just past Hotel
Calipolis is one of the busiest
cruising spots. Prime time is
between 3am and dawn.

L'Atlantida
Shuttle buses take
party-goers to this hugely
popular, summer only, beach
front club. 🅢 Platja les Coves

Privilege
One of the best gay music
bars in town, Privilege has a
different theme every night.
🅢 Carrer de Bonaire 24

El Hotel Romàntic
A simple, gay-friendly hotel,
with a pretty garden. 🅢 C/St
Isidre 33 • 93 894 83 75

The "Gaixample" around the intersection of C/Casanova and
C/Diputació, is the heart of Barcelona's gay scene.

Left **Handbags, Avinguda Diagonal** Right **Shop front, Passeig de Gràcia**

TOP10 Best Shopping Areas

1 Passeig de Gràcia
Barcelona's grand avenue of lavish *Modernista* buildings is fittingly home to the city's premier fashion and design stores. From the international big league (Chanel, Gucci, Swatch) to Spain's heavy hitters (Loewe, Camper, Zara, Mango; *see p139)*, it's all here. And topping the interior design list is the perennially popular Vinçon *(see p106)*. Side streets reveal more sublime shopping, notably Carrer Consell de Cent, which is dotted with art galleries, and carrers Mallorca, València and Roselló. ⊗ *Map E3*

2 Carrer Girona
Looking for fashion bargains? Then head to Carrer Girona (metro Tetuan), which is lined with designer and high-street outlet stores. Most offer women's fashions, including streetwear from brands such as Mango, evening wear and shoes from Catalan designers

Etxart & Panno, and upmarket designs from the likes of Javier Simorra. ⊗ *Map P1*

3 Plaça de Catalunya & Carrer Pelai
The city's booming centrepiece is also its commercial cross-roads, flanked by the department store El Corte Inglés and the shopping mall El Triangle, which includes FNAC (books, CDs, videos) and Séphora (perfumes and cosmetics). Lined with shoe and clothing shops, the nearby Carrer Pelai is said to have more pedestrian traffic than any other shopping street in Spain. ⊗ *El Corte Inglés: Pl de Catalunya 14 • Map M1 • Open 9:30am–9:30pm Mon–Sat* ⊗ *El Triangle: C/Pelai 39 • Map L1 • Open 10am–10pm Mon–Sat*

4 Portal de l'Àngel
Once a Roman thoroughfare leading into the walled city of Barcino, today the pedestrian street of Portal de l'Àngel is traversed by hordes of shoppers toting bulging bags. The street is chock-full of shoe, clothing, jewellery and accessory shops. ⊗ *Map M2*

5 Rambla de Catalunya
The genteel, classier extension of La Rambla, this well-maintained

Shopping crowds, Portal de l'Àngel

street offers a refreshing change from its cousin's more downmarket carnival atmosphere. Chic shops and cafés, as well as their moneyed customers, pepper the street's length, from Plaça de Catalunya to Diagonal. You'll find everything from fine footwear and leather bags to linens and lamps. ◈ *Map E2*

Storefront, Carrer Portaferrissa

Avinguda Diagonal
Big and brash, traffic-choked Diagonal is hard to miss, a cacophonous avenue that cuts, yes, diagonally across the entire city. It is a premier shopping street, particularly west of Passeig de Gràcia to its culmination in L'Illa mall and the large El Corte Inglés department store near Plaça Maria Cristina. Lining this long stretch is a host of high-end clothing and shoe stores (Armani, Loewe and Hugo Boss among them), interior design shops, jewellery and watch purveyors, and more. ◈ *Map D1*

Carrer Portaferrissa
From zebra platform shoes to bellybutton rings and pastel baby T-shirts, this street's other name could well be Carrer "Trendy". In addition to all the usual high-street chains, from H&M to Mango and NafNaf, along this strip you'll find El Mercadillo minimall, crammed with hip little shops selling spiked belts, frameless sunglasses, surf wear and the like. After stocking up on fashions, stop for a box of prettily wrapped chocolates at Fargas, on nearby C/del Pi (No. 16). ◈ *Map M3*

Gràcia
Old bookstores, family-run *botigues de comestibles* (grocery stores) and bohemian shops selling Indian clothing and accessories cluster along Carrer Astúries (and its side streets) and along Travessera de Gràcia. A string of contemporary clothing and shoe shops also lines Gran de Gràcia. ◈ *Map F1*

El Born
Amid El Born's web of streets are all sorts of art and design shops. Passeig del Born and Carrer Rec are dotted with innovative little galleries (from sculpture to interior design), plus clothing and shoe boutiques. This area is by far the best for original fashion and accessories. ◈ *Map P4*

Maremagnum
This shopping centre on the water's edge is open every day of the year, including Sundays. All of the main clothing chains can be found here, along with a variety of cafés and restaurants.
◈ *Muelle de España 5 • Map N5*
• *Open 10am–10pm daily*

Produce, Mercat de Santa Caterina

Most Fascinating Markets

1 Mercat de La Boqueria

Barcelona's most famous food market is conveniently located on La Rambla *(see pp12–13)*. Freshness reigns supreme and shoppers are spoiled for choice, with hundreds of stalls selling everything from vine-ripened tomatoes to haunches of beef and moist wedges of Manchego cheese. The city's seaside status is in full evidence at the fish stalls. ❧ *La Rambla 91 • Map L3 • Open 8am–8pm Mon–Sat*

2 Els Encants

Barcelona's best flea market, Els Encants (east of the city) is where you'll find everything from second-hand clothes, electrical appliances and toys to home-made pottery and used books. Discerning browsers can fit out an entire kitchen from an array of pots and pans. Bargain-hunters should come early. The market is due to relocate nearby in 2013. ❧ *Pl de les Glòries Catalanes • Map H3 • Open 8am–5:30pm Mon, Wed, Fri & Sat*

3 Fira de Santa Llúcia

The Christmas season is officially under way when local artisans set up shop outside the Cathedral for the annual Christmas fair. Well worth a visit if only to peruse the row upon row of *caganers*, miniature figures squatting to *fer caca* (take a poop). Uniquely Catalan, the *caganers* are usually hidden in the back of nativity scenes. This unusual celebration of the scatological also appears in other Christmas traditions. ❧ *Pl de la Seu • Map N3 • Open 1–23 Dec: 10am–8pm (times may vary) daily*

4 Book & Coin Market at Mercat de Sant Antoni

For book lovers, there's no better way to spend Sunday morning than browsing at this market south of La Rambla. You'll find a mind-boggling assortment of weathered paperbacks, ancient tomes, stacks of old magazines, comics, postcards and lots more, from coins to videos. ❧ *C/Comte d'Urgell • Map D2 • Open 8am–3pm Sun*

Fira de Santa Llúcia, Plaça de la Seu

5 Fira Artesana, Plaça del Pi

The Plaça del Pi *(see p37)* brims with natural and organic foods during the Fira Artesana, when producers bring their goods to this corner of the Barri Gòtic. The market specializes in home-made cheeses and honey – from clear clover honey from the Pyrenees to nutty concoctions from Morella. ◈ *Pl del Pi • Map M3 • Open 10am–9pm 1st & 3rd Fri, Sat & Sun of month*

Cheeses, Fira Artesana, Plaça del Pi

6 Fira de Filatelia i Numismàtica

Spread out in the elegant Plaça Reial *(see p72)*, this popular stamp and coin market draws avid collectors from all over the city. The newest collectors' items are phone cards and old *xapes de cava* (cava bottle cork foils). When the market ends (and the local police go to lunch), a makeshift flea market takes over. Old folks from the barrio and immigrants haul out their belongings – old lamps, clothing, junk – and lay it all out on cloths on the ground. ◈ *Pl Reial • Map L4 • Open 9am–2:30pm Sun*

7 Mercat de Barceloneta

The striking Barceloneta covered market overlooks an expansive square. In addition to colourful produce stalls, there is a good restaurant, Els Fogons de la Barceloneta. ◈ *Pl Font 1, Barceloneta • Map F6 • Open 7am–3pm Mon–Thu & Sat, 7am–8pm Fri*

8 Mercat de Santa Caterina

Each barri has its own food market with tempting displays but this one boasts a spectacular setting. The building was designed by Catalan architect Enric Miralles (1955–2000). ◈ *Av Francesc Cambó 16 • Map N3 • Open 7:30am–2pm Mon, 7:30am–3:30pm Tue, Wed & Sat, 7:30am–8:30pm Thu & Fri*

9 Mercat del Art de la Plaça de Sant Josep Oriol

At weekends, local artists flock to this Barri Gòtic square to sell their art and set up their easels. You'll find everything from watercolours of Catalan landscapes to oil paintings of churches and castles. ◈ *Pl de Sant Josep Oriol • Map M4 • Open 11am–8:30pm Sat, 10am–3pm Sun*

10 Mercat dels Antiquaris

Antiques aficionados and collectors contentedly rummage through jewellery, watches, candelabras, embroidery and bric-a-brac at this long-running antiques market in front of the Cathedral. ◈ *Pl de la Seu • Map N3 • Open 10am–9pm Thu (except Aug)*

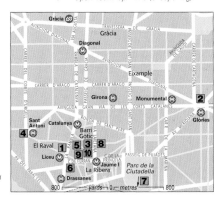

Left **City vista, Mirador de Colom** Right **Gargoyles and view, Sagrada Família**

🔟 City Views

1 Tibidabo

The mountain of Tibidabo is the best vantage point for a bird's-eye view of Barcelona. Thrill-seekers opt for a spin on the Tibidabo fairground attraction *(see p111)* called La Atalaya, a rickety basket attached to an ancient crane-like contraption which gives a 360-degree view of Barcelona, the sea and the Pyrenees. A less giddy option is the Torre de Collserola *(see p111)* with its transparent lift rising up 288 m (945 ft). And for those who wish to keep their feet firmly on solid ground – cocktail in hand – settle in at the Mirablau bar. *See p116.*

2 Castell de Montjuïc

Montjuïc offers myriad view-points. The best is from the castle and gardens with their superb panoramas over the port and the city. Take the cable car up to the castle and walk down through ever-changing vistas to the Font del Gat café to enjoy a cool drink in its romantic gardens. *See p89.*

Barcelona from Castell de Montjuïc

3 Les Golondrines & Orsom Catamaran

The sea offers a less vertiginous view of the cityscape. Glide out of the harbour on the pleasure boats known as *golondrines* or try the exhilarating trip under sail on an enormous catamaran. Both trips offer ample views of the city and of the Port Olímpic area *(see p133).* ⌖ *Les Golondrines, Moll de Drassanes • Map L6 • Call 93 442 31 06 for times • www.lasgolondrinas. com* ⌖ *Orsom Catamaran, Portal de la Pau • Map L6 • Call 93 441 05 37 for times • www.barcelona-orsom.com*

4 Cable Cars

The swaying cable cars that glide slowly between the Port and Montjuïc are something of a Barcelona landmark. To those not afraid of heights, they reveal hidden aspects of the city and provide a pleasurable way to get to Montjuïc *(see p133)* in a 5-minute trip. ⌖ *Miramar, Montjuïc/Port de Barcelona • Map C5, D6 & E6 • Open daily Apr, May & Oct: 10am–7pm; Jun–Sep: 10am–9pm; Nov–Mar: 10am–6pm • Adm*

5 Mirador de Colom

At the end of La Rambla, the statue of Christopher Columbus offers a good vantage point for viewing the city. The column, rising 80 m (262 ft), was built in 1888. The elevator that whisks visitors to the top has, fortunately, been renovated since then! ⌖ *La Rambla/Drassanes • Map L6 • Closed for renovation until further notice • Adm*

Sagrada Família

When work first began, Gaudí's magical church lay on the outskirts of the city and Barcelona would have been just a shadow in the distance. Almost a hundred years on, the church is located in the heart of the Eixample and the bell towers offer dizzying vistas of the entire city. An added bonus are the wonderful close-ups of the extraordinary Sagrada Família itself. *See pp8–11.*

View of the city and Casa-Museu Gaudí, Parc Güell

El Corte Inglés

The top floor of this department store has a glass-fronted cafeteria and restaurant – an excellent place to lunch or just have a coffee. From here there are views of the nearby Plaça de Catalunya, the old town and the Eixample. The enormous store below stocks just about anything you might need to buy. ✪ *Pl de Catalunya 14 • Map M1 • Free • DA*

Parc Güell

In the north of the city, Gaudí's monumental *Modernista* park presents spectacular views across Barcelona and out to the Mediterranean from its various terraced levels. Trees and patches of woodland act as welcome shade from the fierce summer sun. *See p112.*

Barcelona Cathedral

From the heart of the Barri Gòtic, the Cathedral rooftop offers one of the least changed vistas in the city. Look out over the ramshackle rooftops – some dating to the 12th century – and the narrow alleys that spill out in all directions. There is a small charge for the elevator to the top. *See pp14–15.*

Helicopter Rides

For a bird's-eye view of Barcelona, consider a helicopter ride over the city. Cat Helicopters run tours of between five and 35 minutes over the city and as far as Montserrat. The 5-minute tour over the port area costs €50 per person (maximum five people for each journey). ✪ *Moll Adossat s/n • Map D6 • Call 93 224 07 10 or check www.cathelicopters.com for more information • Adm*

Left **Barceloneta beach** Right **Parc de Joan Miró**

🔟 Parks & Beaches

Parc de la Ciutadella

Barcelona's largest land-scaped park offers a serene antidote to city life. Once the location of the 18th-century military citadel, this lovely 19th-century park is now home to the zoo, the Catalan parliament, a museum and a boating lake. There is an attractive outdoor café next to the Castell dels Tres Dracs (in the southwestern corner). *See pp16–17.*

Parc Güell

Originally conceived as a suburban estate to the north of the city, Parc Güell is like a surreal, Asian terraced farm. Twisting pathways and avenues of columned arches blend in with the hillside, playfully fusing nature and fantasy. The esplanade, with its stunning, curved, mosaic bench, is the park's centrepiece. From here

Cascade Fountain, Parc de la Ciutadella

there are spectacular views *(see p55)* of the entire city and of the fairy-tale gatehouses below. Gaudí's former home is now the Casa-Museu Gaudí. *See p112.*

Jardins del Laberint d'Horta

These enchanting Neo-Classical gardens date back to 1791, making this elegant park one of the oldest in the city. Situated up above the city, where the air is cooler and cleaner, the park includes themed gardens, waterfalls and a small canal. The highlight is the enormous maze, which has a statue of Eros at its centre. *See p113.*

Parc de Cervantes

Built in 1964 to celebrate 25 years of Franco rule, this beautiful park on the outskirts of town would have been more appropriately named Park of the Roses. There are over 11,000 rose bushes of 245 varieties; when in bloom, their aroma pervades the park. People pour in at weekends, but the park is blissfully deserted during the week. 🕲 *Av Diagonal 708 • Off map*

Jardins del Palau de Pedralbes

These picturesque gardens lie just in front of the former Palau Reial (royal palace) of Pedralbes. Under the shade of an enormous eucalyptus tree and near a small bamboo forest is a fountain with a dragon head by Gaudí, which

All the city parks are officially open from around 10am until dusk.

Parc de Joan Miró

Also know as Parc de l'Escorxador, this park was built on the site of a 19th-century slaughter-house (*excorxador*). Dominating the paved upper level of the park is Miró's striking 22-m (72-ft) sculpture,

Parc de l'Espanya Industrial

Dona i Ocell (Woman and Bird; 1983). Elsewhere there are several children's play areas and a couple of kiosk cafés. • *C/Tarragona 74 • Map B2*

Parc de l'Espanya Industrial

Located on the site of a former textiles factory, this modern park was built by Basque architect Luis Peña Ganchegui. It's a very appealing space, with ten strange lighthouse-style towers that line the boating lake and an enormous cast-iron dragon, which doubles as a slide. There's a good terrace bar with a playground for the kids. • *C/Muntades 37 • Off map*

City Beaches

The beaches of Barcelona were once insalubrious areas to be avoided. With the 1992 Olympics they underwent a radical face-lift and today the stretches of Barceloneta and the Port Olímpic are a major people magnet. Just a short hop on the metro from the city centre, they provide the perfect opportunity for a refreshing Mediterranean dip. The beaches are regularly cleaned and the many facilities

include showers, toilets, childrens' play areas, volleyball nets and an open-air gym. There are boats and surfboards for rent. Be warned: bag snatching is endemic. *See p97.*

Castelldefels

Just 20 km (12 miles) south of Barcelona are 5 km (3 miles) of wide, sandy beaches with shallow waters. Beach bars entice weekend sun worshippers out of the afternoon sun for long, lazy seafood lunches and jugs of sangria aplenty. Windsurfers and pedalos are for hire. • *Off map • Train to Platja de Castelldefels from Estació de Sants or Passeig de Gràcia*

Premià/El Masnou

Arguably the best beaches within easy reach of Barcelona, just 20 km (12 miles) to the north, these two adjoining beaches lure locals with gorgeous golden sand and clear, blue waters. • *Train to Premià or El Masnou from Plaça de Catalunya or Estació de Sants*

Left **La Rambla** Right **Cyclist, Passeig Marítim**

🔟 Walks & Bike Rides

1 La Rambla & The Port
From Plaça de Catalunya, stroll the length of Barcelona's most famous street, La Rambla *(see pp12–13)*, stopping en route to enjoy the street performances. Turn left at the port and admire the luxury yachts as you follow the water round to Barceloneta. Continue along Pg Joan de Borbó and turn left down any of the side streets that lead to the sand and sea. 🗺 Map M1

2 Barri Gòtic
Wandering this network of atmospheric, ancient streets is the best way to experience the old town. Take a short stretch of the busy C/Portaferrisa *(see p51)* from La Rambla and turn right down tiny C/Petritxol *(see p74)*, with its confectionery shops and jewellers, to the Església de Santa Maria del Pi. Continue down C/Rauric, left onto C/Ferran and up to Plaça de Sant Jaume *(see p71)*. Turn left onto C/Bisbe leading to Plaça de la Seu and the Cathedral *(see pp14–15)*. 🗺 Map L3

3 Eixample
For some of the city's most breathtaking *Modernista* gems, walk the length of Pg de Gràcia south to north, past the Mansana de la Discòrdia *(see p103)* and La Pedrera *(see pp20–21)*. Turn right onto C/Mallorca, which leads to Gaudí's Sagrada Família *(see pp 8–11)*. Take a left along C/Marina, past the church's awe-inspiring Nativity Façade, and head up Av Gaudí to Hospital de la Santa Creu i de Sant Pau *(see p103)*. 🗺 Map E3

4 Tibidabo
Get high above the city by following the gently climbing Av del Tibidabo from the FGC station. Then follow signposts to the right through the steep wooded park, Font del Racó, and continue until you arrive at Plaça Doctor Andreu with its terrace bars and panoramic city views. 🗺 Map B1

5 Montjuïc
Take in the city's green scene with an amble around Montjuïc's

Parc de Collserola

The CCCB (see pp28–9) offers occasional guided walks in English during the year. For more on walking tours **See p133.**

verdant slopes. The initial climb to the grandiose Palau Nacional *(see pp18–19)* from Plaça d'Espanya is eased by a series of escalators. From the palace, veer left and continue along the

Backstreet, Barri Gòtic

main road, stopping off at Jardí Mossèn Jacint Verdaguer *(see p94)* before continuing round to Miramar for a spectacular view. ⊗ *Map B3*

Parc de Collserola
It's difficult to believe that this serene nature reserve lies just 10 minutes drive from the metropolis. Explore its delightful hiking, biking and nature trails on foot or by mountain bike. Take the FGC train to Baixador de Vallvidrera and follow the signs to the park information office, where you will find maps, advice on routes and a charming café. ⊗ *Tourist Info: Carretera de Vallvidrera a Sant Cugat, km 4.7 • Open 9:30am–3pm daily*

Coastal Bike Ride
Breeze along the city's coastal cycle path and take in seaside Barcelona. Pick up the path from the bottom of La Rambla and follow it north to Barceloneta, where it runs along the beachfront, past the shiny Port Olímpic as far as the Platja Levant. ⊗ *Map B3*

Diagonal Bike Ride
From Pedralbes to the sea, this route along the city's most elegant boulevard gives you a clear idea of Barcelona's size. The tree-lined cycle path follows Diagonal; start at the top (Zona Universitària) and continuing through the new city of Diagonal Mar until you arrive on the other

side of the city just a stone's throw from the Besòs River. ⊗ *Map A1*

Les Planes
Just a 15-minute *ferrocarril* ride from Plaça de Catalunya (in the direction of Sant Cugat) is the picturesque spot of Baixador de Valvidrera. Perfect for an out-of-town stroll, there is a steep path through the woods, which opens up into a beautiful, green valley. In summer, there are barbecue facilities where you can throw on your own steaks. ⊗ *4 km N of Barcelona*

Costa Brava Coastal Path
At the end of the Platja de Sant Pol in Sant Feliu de Guíxols is the start of a beautiful, coastal path that winds north through shady tamarind trees with views of rocky coves and the Mediterranean. Around the headland and down a stairway, you will find the fabulous beach of Sa Conca, said to be one of the best in Spain. ⊗ *75 km NE of Barcelona*

Bike rental is available from Budget Bikes in Calle Estruc 38 (tel: 93 304 18 85). For more on bike rental **See p131 & p133.**

59

Left **Bernat Picornell outdoor pool** Right **Sunbathers, Platja de la Barceloneta**

Activities in Barcelona

Sunbathing & Swimming
Head to the city beaches *(see p57)* to cool down and escape the stifling heat. Barcelona boasts a wide range of fabulous beaches, from Barceloneta, lined with bars and restaurants, to the reclaimed beaches of Vila Olímpica, Bogatell and Mar Bella. ◈ *Map F6–H6*

Watersports
A wide variety of activities is on offer in the jet-set surroundings of Port Olímpic and neighbouring beaches, including dinghy sailing and windsurfing. For the experienced, boats are available for hire from the Escola Municipal de Vela; for the beginner, there are classes.
◈ *Escola Municipal de vela • Moll de Gregal • Map G6 • 93 225 79 40 • Open 9:30am–8pm daily*

Volleyball, Platja de Nova Icària

Swimming
Set in the green environs of Montjuïc, the outstanding outdoor pool of Bernat Picornell is surprisingly uncrowded, especially in summer. It has sun loungers, an ice-cream stall and a huge electronic timer with which swimmers in training or fitness enthusiasts can time their sprints. In 2013 it will host some of the events in the World Aquatics Championships.
◈ *Av del Estadi 30 • Map A4 • 93 423 40 41 • Open 7am–midnight Mon–Fri, 7am–9pm Sat, 7:30am–8pm Sun • Adm • DA*

Pitch-&-Putt Golf
The Costa Brava is emerging as one of Spain's top golf destinations but if you're looking to tee off in town, your best bets are the nearby pitch-and-putt courses in Badalona and Castelldefells.
◈ *Castell de Godmar, Pomar de Dalt 13, Badalona, 5km NE Barcelona • 93 395 27 79 • Open 8:30am–dusk daily* ◈ *Canal Olímpic • Castell-defels, 20 km S Barcelona • 93 636 28 96 • Open 9am–9pm Tue–Sat (to 8pm Sun)*

Beach Volleyball
On weekend mornings year-round you can pick up a volleyball game at Platja de la Nova Icària. It is best to go with enough people to form a team, but you are usually welcome to join in an ongoing game. ◈ *Map H5*

Horse Riding
The municipal riding school, *Escola Municipal d'Hipica La Foixarda*, in Montjuïc offers classes for riders of all levels. An hour-long session is €17 for adults and €14 for children. There are also Shetland ponies for small children (€6 for 30 minutes). Take the Metro Espanya and then bus number 50. It is based in La Fuixarda, which is also a popular climbing venue. ◈ *Av Muntanyans 1, Montjuïc • Map B4 • 93 426 10 66 • Open 5:30–8pm Mon–Fri, 9am–1:30pm, 5–7pm Sat & Sun*

Biking

Hire a bike from Barcelona Biking and breeze around the city. Alternatively, opt for an electric bike, which can switch from manual to electric whenever you need a little extra push.
Barcelona Biking • Baixada de Sant Miquel 6 • 65 635 63 00 *Barcelona Battery Bikes • C/Sant Felip Neri 1 • 93 301 71 70 • www.barcelonabatterybikes.com*

Tennis

There are tennis courts and clubs all around the city. At the complex used during the 1992 Olympics, you can rent courts by the hour or sign up for lessons.
Barcelona Tennis Olimpic • Passeig de la Vall d'Hebron 178–196 • 93 427 65 00

Sardanes

These traditional Catalan dances *(see p65)* take place regularly all over the city and at most local festas. They often involve up to 200 people, and there's no reason why you can't be one of them.

Frontó

All you need to enjoy this popular pastime is a tennis racket and ball to beat against the wall. The city's parks are full of free *frontó* courts; one of the most central is called Frontó Colom, at La Rambla 18.

Biking in Barcelona

Top 10 Spectator Sports & Events

1 FC Barcelona Football
Tickets to see this side are rare; book online or by phone.
Sep–Jun • 93 496 36 00/902 18 99 00 • www.fcbarcelona.com

2 RCD Espanyol
It's easier to get tickets for this first-division football side; they play at Estadi del RCD Espanyol *(see p90)*.
Sep–Jun • 93 292 77 00

3 FC Barcelona Basketball
The team of the city's second favourite sport play at the Palau Blaugrana. *Sep–May • 902 18 99 00/93 496 36 00*

4 Barcelona Marató
The marathon takes in the whole city before culminating at the Plaza de España. *early March • www.barcelonamarato.es*

5 Barcelona Open
This tennis tournament attracts some big names.
mid–late Apr • 93 203 78 52

6 Cursa El Corte Inglés
A very popular 11-km (7-mile) run. *Apr or May • www.cursaelcorteingles.cat*

7 La Volta Ciclista de Catalunya
Cyclists warm up for the more serious European events with this testing route.
late Mar–Apr • 93 431 82 98

8 Montmeló
Motor racing, including Formula 1, regularly comes to this circuit. *Apr–May • 93 571 97 00 • www.circuitcat.com*

9 Cursa La Mercè
A 10-km (6-mile) run through Barcelona's centre.
Late Sep • 010

10 Catalunya Rally
Top-class rally-driving in spectacular surroundings.
Oct or Nov • www.rallyracc.com

Left **Children at play, Port Olímpic beach** Right **Penguins, Parc Zoològic**

Attractions for Children

1 Parc d'Atraccions del Tibidabo

With its old-fashioned rides, the only surviving funfair in the city is a delight. The attractions include a rollercoaster, a House of Horrors, bumper cars, a ferris wheel and the Museu dels Autòmates *(see p41)*, with animatronics of all shapes and sizes. There's also a puppet show, picnic areas, playgrounds and plenty of bars and restaurants. *See p111.*

2 Parc Zoològic

The zoo has an enormous adventure playground where children can run wild. There are also dolphin shows in one of the aquariums. Other activities for children include guided tours and workshops. The "farm" area has goats and rabbits that younger children can stroke. *See p16.*

3 Museu Marítim

Ancient maps showing monster-filled seas, restored fishing boats and a collection of ships' figureheads give a taste of Barcelona's maritime history. Well worth a look is the full-size Spanish galleon complete with sound and light effects. Set in the vast former medieval shipyards, the Drassanes, this is an absolute must for any budding sea captain. *See p81.*

4 L'Aquàrium

One of Europe's biggest aquariums, this underwater kingdom is made up of 21 enormous tanks brimming with nearly 400 marine species. The highlight of a visit is the Oceanari, where a walk-through glass tunnel will bring you face to face with three huge grey sharks – named Drake, Morgan and Maverick – lurking in 4.5 million litres (990,000 gallons) of water. *See p97.*

5 Jardins del Laberint d'Horta

The main feature of this exceptional park is the huge, hedged maze where children can live

Children, Parc Zoològic

out their *Alice in Wonderland* fantasies. Unfulfilled expectations of mad hatters are made up for by an enormous play area with a bar and terrace. The park is particularly busy on Sundays. *See p113.*

6 Montjuïc Cable Cars

Unlike the nerve-jangling cable-car ride across the port, these smaller, lower-altitude cable car trips are a better option if you have children with you. The ride to the Montjuïc summit also has the added appeal of the castle *(see p89)* at the top, with cannons for the kids to clamber on. ✪ *Parc de Montjuïc • Map C5 • Open Nov–Feb: 10am–6pm daily; Mar–May, Oct: 10am–7pm daily; Jun–Sep: 10am–9pm daily • Adm • DA*

Human statue, La Rambla

7 La Rambla

Your shoulders will be aching from carrying the kids high above the crowds by the time you reach the end of Barcelona's main boulevard. Fire eaters, buskers, human statues decked out as Greek goddesses – you name it and it's likely to be keeping the hordes entertained on La Rambla. Put a coin in the human statue's hat and be rewarded with a sudden move, or, if you're a child, the gift of a tiny lollipop. *See pp12–13.*

8 City Beaches

For kids, there's more to going to the beach in Barcelona than just splashing in warm waters and frolicking in the sand. The Port Vell and Port Olímpic *platges* (beaches) offer a good choice of well-equipped play areas to keep the little ones entertained. Numerous bars and restaurants make finding refreshment easy, too. *See p97.*

9 Boat Trips

Barcelona's *golondrines* (see p133) make regular trips out of the port, providing a fun excursion for older children. Younger kids, however, will probably prefer paddling around in a rowing boat on the lake at the Parc de la Ciutadella. *See pp16–17.*

10 Museu d'Història de Catalunya

This child-friendly museum traces Catalonia's history through a range of dynamic, interactive exhibits. The best of these allows visitors to get dressed up as medieval knights and gallop around on wooden horses. Very popular with Catalan school groups, it's equally enjoyable for visitors. Every Saturday, the museum hosts a story hour when Catalan legends are re-enacted for children as well as other children's activities. *See p97.*

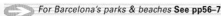

For Barcelona's parks & beaches **See pp56–7**

Festes de la Mercè

Catalan Folk Festivals & Traditions

Festes de la Mercè
Barcelona's main festival is a riotous week-long celebration in honour of La Mercè *(see p39)*. The night sky lights up with fireworks, outdoor concerts are held, and there's barely a bottle of *cava* left in the city by the festival's end. Processions and parades feature *gegants* (giant wooden figures operated by people). ⚲ *Week of 23 Sep*

Gegants, Festes de la Mercè

El Dia de Sant Jordi
On this spring day, Barcelona is transformed into a vibrant, open-air book and flower market. Men and women exchange presents of roses, to celebrate Sant Jordi *(see p39)* and books, in tribute to Cervantes and Shakespeare, who both died on 23 April 1616. ⚲ *23 Apr*

La Revetlla de Sant Joan
In celebration of Saint John, and the start of summer, this is Catalonians' night to play with fire and play they do, with gusto. Fireworks streak through the night sky and bonfires are set ablaze on beaches and in towns throughout the region. ⚲ *23 Jun*

Festa Major de Gràcia
During this week-long *festa*, (the largest party of the summer), revellers congregate in Gràcia's decorated streets. Parades, open-air concerts, fireworks and plenty of beer and cava fuel the infectious merriment. ⚲ *Mid- to late Aug*

Carnaval in Sitges
The buzzing beach town of Sitges *(see p121)* explodes during Carnaval, celebrated in flamboyant fashion. Over-the-top floats parade among drag queens, lip-synching contests and a fresh-off-the-beach crowd warmed by sun and plenty of beer. ⚲ *3–4 days Feb*

Festa de la Patum
The village of Berga (90 km/ 60 miles north of Barcelona) hosts one of Catalonia's liveliest festivals. The event gets its name from the folks who used to chant *pa-tum* (the sound of a drum). Streets spill over with merrymakers as fireworks crackle and dwarfs, devils and dragons dance atop parade floats. ⚲ *Corpus Christi (May)*

Festes de Sant Medir
A 10th-century hermitage is the focus of a very picturesque pilgrimage featuring carriages and costumed attendants on horseback. Sweets are thrown from the carriages, which is a treat for the kids. ⚲ *Around 3 Mar*

The English-language website www.spain.info has a section dedicated to Spanish festivals.

Castells
8 *Castells* is one of Catalonia's most spectacular folk traditions. Trained *castellers* stand on each other's shoulders to create a human castle – the highest tower takes the prize. The crowning moment is when a child scales the human mass to make the sign of the cross. *Castells* are often performed in Plaça Sant Jaume. 🕔 *Jun*

Sardanes
9 "The magnificent, moving ring" is how Catalan poet Joan Maragall described the *sardana*, Catalonia's regional dance. Subdued yet intricate, it is performed to the tunes of the *cobla*, a traditional brass and woodwind band. *Sardanes* can be seen in Plaça de la Seu and Plaça Sant Jaume year round *(see p14)*.

Catalan Christmas & Cavalcada de Reis
10 The *Nadal* (Christmas) season begins on 1 December with the arrival of the festive artisan fairs. On 5 January is the Cavalcada de Reis, the spectacular Three Kings Parade. In Barcelona, the kings arrive by sea and are welcomed by city officials in front of transfixed children.

Castells

Top 10 Music, Theatre & Art Festivals

1 **Grec Festival Barcelona**
Barcelona's largest music, theatre and dance festival.
🕔 *late Jun–Jul* • 93 316 10 00
• www.bcn.cat/grec

2 **Festival del Sónar**
This electronic music and multimedia festival has technology fairs and musical events.
🕔 *mid-Jun* • www.sonar.es

3 **Festival Internacional de Jazz**
Big-name and experimental live jazz. 🕔 *Oct–Nov* • 93 481 70 40 • www.barcelonajazz festival.com

4 **Sitges International Film Festival**
The best fantasy film festival in the world. 🕔 *early Oct*
• http://sitgesfilmfestival.com

5 **Festival de Música Antiga**
Concerts of early music in the Barri Gòtic and L'Auditori.
🕔 *Feb–Jul* • www.auditori.cat

6 **Clàssica als Parcs**
Classical music concerts are held in the city's parks.
🕔 *Jun–Aug* • 010

7 **Festival de Guitarra**
International guitar festival.
🕔 *Feb–Jun* • 93 481 70 40
• www.theproject.es

8 **Festival de Músiques del Món**
Ethnic and world music at L'Auditori. 🕔 *Oct* • www.auditori.cat

9 **Ciutat Flamenco**
A week of outstanding flamenco music at the Mercat de les Flors. 🕔 *late May*
• 93 443 43 46 • www. ciutatflamenco.com

10 **Primavera Sound**
Pop, rock and underground dance music festival with big-name acts. 🕔 *late May*
• www.primaverasound.com

Tickets for the Grec Festival Barcelona & Festival Internacional de Jazz are available from the Telentrada ticket line: 902 10 12 12.

Left **Teatre Grec** Right **Gran Teatre del Liceu**

Performing Arts & Music Venues

1 Gran Teatre del Liceu
Phoenix-like, the Liceu has risen from the ashes of two devastating fires since its inauguration in 1847. Now one of the greatest opera houses in Europe, it has an innovative programme and is famed for performances by home-grown talent, including one of the "three tenors" José Carreras. ✆ *La Rambla • Map L4 • 93 485 99 14 • Guided tours 10am daily, non-guided tours 11:30am, noon, 12:30pm & 1pm daily • Adm • DA*

2 El Molino
El Molino has been a musical theatre-bar since 1907. It hosts music, cabaret shows, flamenco and tango performances. Book through the website. ✆ *Vila i Vila 99 (Av. Paral.lel) • 93 205 51 11 • Adm • DA • www.elmolinobcn.com*

3 Teatre Grec
The most magical and enigmatic of all Barcelona's venues, this open-air amphitheatre, set in thick, verdant forest, makes an incredible setting for ballet,

music or theatre. Only used for shows during the summer arts Grec Festival, the gardens are open all year to visitors. *See p90.* ✆ *Tickets: 902 10 12 12 • Open for visits 10am–dusk daily • Free*

4 Palau de la Música Catalana
Domènech i Montaner's *Modernista* gem regularly serves up the best in jazz and classical music. It has lost some of its prestige to the Auditori, but it still hosts some performances for the annual guitar festival and attracts many visiting world music artists. *See pp26–7.*

5 Auditori de Barcelona
Located near the Teatre Nacional, this large auditorium is home to the Orquestra Simfònica de Barcelona and also houses the Museum of Music. Acoustics and visibility are excellent and, in addition to classical music, it hosts regular jazz concerts. ✆ *C/Lepant 150 • Map G1 • 93 247 93 00 • DA*

6 Harlem Jazz Club
This is one of the longest surviving clubs for jazz and blues. Admission usually includes a drink, and some shows are free. *See p77.* ✆ *93 310 07 55 • www. harlemjazzclub.es*

Concert, Palau de la Música Catalana

For Catalan speakers, the Teatre Nacional de Catalunya (93 306 57 00) is a fine showcase for Catalan drama.

7 Mercat de les Flors

The venue of choice for dance and performance theatre groups, such as La Fura dels Baus and Comediants, whose incredible mixture of circus and drama is easily accessible to non-Catalan speakers. ⚲ C/Lleida 59 • Map B4 • 93 426 18 75 • www.mercatflors.cat

8 Sala Apolo

An old dance hall, with velvet covered balconies and panelled bars, this place has reinvented itself as one of the city's leading nightclubs. It attracts the latest in live techno and dance music. ⚲ C/Nou de la Rambla 113 • Map K4 • 93 441 40 01 • www.sala-apolo.com

Harlem Jazz Club

9 JazzSí Club – Taller de Musics

Conceived as a multi-functional space, the JazzSí Club offers music workshops, lessons and daily concerts in the auditorium. The jazz, Cuban, flamenco or rock performances start between 7:30 (6:30 on Sun) and 9pm, and dinner is available from Monday to Friday. ⚲ Requesens, 2 • Map J2 • 93 329 00 20 • www.tallerdemusics.com/jazzsi-club/ • Adm

10 Razzmatazz

This is one of the city's most famous venues. Hosting concerts several nights a week, the club's five areas offer a wide range of musical styles. *See p100.*

Top 10 Versión Original Cinemas

1 Verdi

One of the original VO cinemas, with five screens. ⚲ C/Verdi 32 • Map B2 • 93 238 79 90 • www.cines-verdi.com

2 Icària Yelmo Cineplex

An incredible 15 screens showing VO films. ⚲ C/Salvador Espriu 61 • Map H5 • 902 22 09 22 • www.yelmocines.com

3 Festival de Cine Documental Musical In-Edit

This festival celebrates music and film. ⚲ late Oct–early Nov • www.in-edit.beefeater.es

4 Festival Internacional de Cinema Catalunya

Original version films are screened during this October festival. ⚲ Sitges • 93 894 99 90

5 Méliès Cinemes

Two-screened repertory cinema. ⚲ C/Villarroel 102 • Map J1 • 93 451 00 51

6 Festival Internacional de Cine de Autor

This independent film festival is hosted by the Filmoteca. ⚲ late Apr–early May • www.cinemadautor.cat

7 Verdi Park

Four-screen version of the original Verdi. ⚲ C/Torrijos 49 • Map F1 • 93 238 79 90

8 Renoir Floridablanca

A multiplex that shows films from around the world. ⚲ Floridablanca 135 • Map C3 • 93 426 33 37

9 Sala Montjuic

This outdoor cinema near the castle shows subtitled cult films in summer. ⚲ Montjuic • Map B6 • www.salamontjuic.org

10 Filmoteca

The Catalan government's repertory cinema runs three VO shows daily. ⚲ C/Salvador Seguí 1–9 • 93 567 10 70

Barcelona's many versió original (original version) cinemas provide plenty of options for non-Catalan-speaking film aficionados.

AROUND TOWN

BARCELONA'S TOP 10

Left **Museu d'Història de Barcelona** Right **Saló de Cent, Ajuntament**

Barri Gòtic & La Ribera

THOUGH HARD TO IMAGINE TODAY, *there was a time when Barcelona was just a small Roman village (named Barcino) encircled by protective stone walls. Over the centuries, the village grew, culminating in a building boom in the 14th and 15th centuries. The Barri Gòtic (Gothic Quarter), a beautifully preserved neighbourhood of Gothic buildings, medieval places (squares) and atmospheric alleys, exists today as a splendid reminder of Barcelona's medieval heyday. The web of ancient, treasure-filled streets in this compact area is best explored by aimless wandering. The barri's centrepiece – and its religious and social heart – is the 13th-century Cathedral and surrounding complex of period buildings. Nearby, the stately Plaça del Rei (see p36) is ringed by some of the best preserved medieval buildings in the area. Extending east of the Barri Gòtic is the ancient barri of La Ribera, which includes El Born (see p72). Here, the lovely Carrer Montcada is lined with medieval palaces – five of which house the must-see Museu Picasso.*

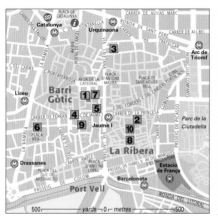

Roman Arch, Carrer Paradis

Sights

1. Barcelona Cathedral
2. Museu Picasso
3. Palau de la Música Catalana
4. Plaça de Sant Jaume
5. Conjunt Monumental de la Plaça del Rei
6. Plaça Reial
7. Museu Frederic Marès
8. Església de Santa Maria del Mar
9. Museu d'Idees i d'Invents (MiBa)
10. Museo de las Culturas del Mundo

For sights & attractions on La Rambla See pp12–13

1. Barcelona Cathedral

Soaring over the Barri Gòtic is Barcelona's mighty Cathedral dating from 1298. *See pp14–15.*

2. Museu Picasso

Discover the youthful repertoire of one of the 20th-century's most revered artists. *See pp24–5.*

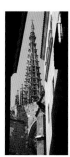

Cathedral spire

3. Palau de la Música Catalana

The city's most prestigious concert hall is a monument to both *la musica Catalana* and to *Modernisme. See pp26–7.*

4. Plaça de Sant Jaume

The site of the Plaça de Sant Jaume *(see p36)* was once the nucleus of Roman Barcino. With these roots, it seems fitting that the square has become home to Barcelona's two most important government buildings: the Palau de la Generalitat (seat of the Catalan government) and the Ajuntament (city hall). Look for the detailed carved relief of Sant Jordi, Catalonia's patron saint, on the 15th-century Generalitat façade. Within is the lovely 15th-century Capella de Sant Jordi *(see p39)*. A highlight of the Gothic Ajuntament is the Saló de Cent, where the Council of One Hundred ruled the city from 1372 to 1714. Also of

note is the Pati dels Tarongers, a patio with orange trees. ✆ *Palau de la Generalitat • Pl de Sant Jaume • Map M4 • 012 (within the city) • Open 10:30am–1:30pm 2nd & 4th Sat & Sun of month for guided tours, adv booking essential on www.president.cat/pres_gov/ president/ca/presidencia/palau-generalitat/visites.html • Free* ✆ *Ajuntament • Pl de Sant Jaume • Open 10am–1:30pm Sun for guided tours (11am English) • Free*

5. Conjunt Monumental de la Plaça del Rei

In the heart of the Barri Gòtic is the beautiful medieval Plaça del Rei *(see p36)*, presided over by the 13th- to 14th-century Palau Reial (royal palace). The impressive palace complex includes the Saló del Tinell, a massive hall crowned by Gothic arches, where Ferdinand and Isabel welcomed Columbus after his 1492 voyage to the Americas. The medieval Capella de Santa Àgata has a beautiful 15th-century altarpiece by Jaume Huguet. A visit to the Museu d'Història de Barcelona gives access to the Palau Reial and to one of the largest underground excavations of Roman ruins on display in Europe. ✆ *Pl del Rei • Map M4 • Open 10am–7pm Tue–Sat, 10am–8pm Sun • Adm; free 1st Sun of month and 3–8pm every Sun • DA*

Left **Italianate façade, Palau de la Generalitat** Right **Mosaic pillar, Palau de la Música Catalana**

For more on Barri Gòtic squares **See pp36–7**

El Born

If you're hankering for a proper martini or perhaps some alternative jazz, then look no further than El Born, a musty-turned-hip neighbourhood, which was "reborn" several years ago. Students and artists moved in, attracted by cheap rents and airy warehouses, fostering an arty vibe that now blends in with the area's old-time aura. Experimental design shops share the narrow streets with traditional, balconied buildings strung with laundry. The bustling Passeig de Born, lined with bars and cafés, leads onto the lively Plaça Comercial, where the cavernous Born Market (in operation 1870–1970) has now been converted into a cultural centre and exhibition space.

Plaça Reial (1850s)

Plaça Reial

Late 19th-century elegance meets sangria-swilling café society in the arcaded Plaça Reial, one of Barcelona's most emblematic and entertaining squares. The *plaça* is planted with towering palm trees and encircled by stately, 19th-century buildings. The *Modernista* lampposts were designed by a young Gaudí in 1879. At the square's centre is a wrought-iron fountain representing the Three Graces. The square is the best place to start a big night out, with a cluster of restaurants, bars and cafés that draw the hoi polloi – including all sorts of shady pickpockets. ◈ *Map L4*

Museu Frederic Marès

This fascinating museum houses the life collection of wealthy Catalan sculptor Frederic

Medieval arch, Museu Frederic Marès

Marès. No mere hobby collector, the astute (and obsessive) Marès amassed holdings that a modern museum curator would die for. Among them, an impressive array of religious icons and statues – dating from Roman times to the present – and the curious "Museu Sentimental", which displays anything from ancient watches to fans and dolls. Also worth a visit during summer is Cafè d'Estiu *(see p78)*, a sunny spot for a snack on the museum's patio. ◈ *Pl de Sant Iu 5–6 • Map N3 • Open 10am–7pm Tue–Sat, 11am–8pm Sun • Adm (free first Sun of the month and 3–8pm every Sun) • DA*

Església de Santa Maria del Mar

The spacious, breathtaking interior of this 14th-century church, designed by architect Berenguer de Montagut, is the city's premier example of the austere Catalan Gothic style. The church is dedicated to Saint Mary of the Sea, the patron saint of sailors, and an ancient model ship hangs near one of the statues of the Virgin. Dubbed "the people's church", this is the city's most popular spot for exchanging wedding vows. ◈ *Pl de Santa Maria 1 • Map P5 • Open 9am–1:30pm, 4:30–8pm*

9 Museu d'Idees i d'Invents (MiBa)

This small private museum, the brainchild of local TV personality Pep Torres, is full of fascinating items – some amusing (a mug with a shelf for biscuits), others truly groundbreaking (the self-regulatory glasses). Temporary exhibitions take place upstairs, while the permanent collection is in the lower gallery (reached by a tube slide). Children are encouraged to submit their designs, the best of which are patented and produced.

Ⓢ C/Ciutat 7 • Map N4 • 93 332 79 30 • Open 10am–2pm & 4–7pm Tue–Fri, 11am–8pm Sat, 10am–2pm Sun • Adm • www.mibamuseum.com

10 Museo de las Culturas del Mundo

The World Culture Museum is due to open in June 2014 in the 16th-century Nadal and Marqués de Lió palaces. Around 700 artistic works are to be displayed, offering a journey through the cultures of Asia, Africa, America and Oceania.

Ⓢ C/Montcada 14 • Map P4 • Check opening hours in advance of your visit • Adm • DA

Interior, Església de Santa Maria del Mar

Roman Barcelona

Morning

🕙 Starting at the Jaume I metro, enter the ancient walled city of Barcino on C/Llibreteria, once the main road to and from Rome. Head right up C/Veguer to **Plaça del Rei** (see p36) and descend into a fascinating underground web of Roman walls and waterways via the **Museu d'Història de Barcelona** (see p71). Also visible here are the remains of a 2nd-century workshop and an ancient bodega, a source of much Roman merrymaking. Back above ground, pause for a cafè sol at the terrace of **Café-Bar L'Antiquari** (see p78) and bask in Barcelona's Gothic glory days. Stroll towards the Cathedral's spires along C/de la Pietat. Turn right onto C/Bisbe, once a Roman thoroughfare, then right again on Av de la Catedral to visit the **Pia Almoina** (see p15), where you can view a section of the Roman aqueduct and ride a glass elevator past Roman wall remains. Backtrack to Plaça Nova, once the Roman gateway to Barcino, cross the plaça and continue along C/Arcs.

Afternoon

📍 Stop for lunch at the **Reial Cercle Artístic**, a late 19th-century artists' society. Ignore the "members only" sign; the restaurant is open to the public, and its tranquil balcony terrace provides a welcome breather from the crowds far below. After lunch, head up Av del Portal de l'Àngel and turn left onto C/Canuda to **Plaça de la Vila de Madrid** (see p37). The square is a fitting end to your Roman ramble, for here are the necropolis remains, where Romans were laid to rest.

Left **Carrer del Bisbe** Centre **Església de Sant Just i Sant Pastor** Right **Plaça de Sant Felip Neri**

TOP10 Best of the Rest

1 Carrer del Bisbe

Medieval Carrer del Bisbe is flanked by the Gothic Cases dels Canonges (House of Canons) and the Palau de la Generalitat (see p71). Connecting the two is an eye-catching Neo-Gothic arched stone bridge (1928). ✆ Map M3

2 Carrer de Santa Llúcia

At weekends, amateur opera singers perform on this medieval street, home to the Casa de l'Ardiaca (see p15), which has a ravishing little patio. ✆ Map M3

3 El Call

El Call was home to one of Spain's largest Jewish communities until their expulsion in the 15th century. Inside the shop at Carrer de Banys Nous 10, you can view the ancient Jewish baths for men. ✆ Map M4

4 Carrer Montcada

The "palace row" of La Ribera is lined with Gothic architectural gems, including the 15th-century Palau Aguilar, home to the Museu Picasso (see pp24–5), and the 17th-century Palau Dalmases with its Gothic chapel. ✆ Map P4

5 Plaça de Ramon Berenguer el Gran

This square boasts one of the largest intact sections of Barcelona's Roman walls. ✆ Map N3

6 Carrer Regomir & Carrer del Correu Vell

You'll find splendid Roman remains on Carrer Regomir, most notably within the medieval Pati Llimona. Two Roman towers are revealed on nearby Carrer del Correu Vell, and there are Roman walls on the leafy Plaça Traginers. ✆ Map M5

7 Plaça de Sant Felip Neri

Sunlight filters through tall trees in this hidden oasis of calm. The plaça is home to the Museu del Calçat (see p41). ✆ Map M3

8 Carrer Petritxol

This well-maintained medieval street is lined with traditional granges and xocolateries (cafés and chocolate shops). Also here is the famous Sala Parés art gallery, founded in 1877, which once exhibited Picasso, Casas and other Catalan contemporaries. ✆ Map L3

9 Església de Sant Just i Sant Pastor

This Gothic church (1342) has sculptures dating back to the 9th century, and 5th-century visigothic baptismal fonts. ✆ Map M4

10 Església de Santa Anna

Mere paces from La Rambla is the unexpected tranquillity of this Romanesque church, with a leafy, 15th-century, Gothic cloister. ✆ Map M2

Left **Escribà Confiteria i Fleca** Centre **La Manual Alpargatera** Right **Guantería Alonso**

Shops: Gifts, Garments & Goodies

1 Escribà Confiteria i Fleca
If the glistening pastries and towering chocolate creations aren't enough of a lure, then the *Modernista* store-front certainly is. Buy goodies to go, or enjoy them on the spot in the small café. ◈ *La Rambla 83 • Map L3*

2 Como Agua de Mayo
Try this tiny boutique for original fashion and footwear by Spanish designers. The style is feminine and glamorous and the prices are surprisingly affordable. ◈ *C/Argenteria 43 • Map N4*

3 Coquette
Divine women's fashions, accessories and toiletries are found in this loft-style store. Among the labels are top Spanish and French names, such as Hoss, Intropia and See by Chloé. ◈ *C/Rec 65 • Map P5*

4 Galeria Antic & Modern
Original artworks, design objects and antiques are on sale at this gallery and shop located under the arcades of a Gothic building. ◈ *C/Rec 50 • Map P4*

5 La Manual Alpargatera
What do the Pope, Jack Nicholson and legions of *Barcelonins* have in common? They buy their espadrilles (*alpargatas*) here. ◈ *C/Avinyó 7 • Map M4*

6 Casa Colomina
Sink your teeth into *torró*, the Spanish nougat-and-almond speciality. Casa Colomina, established in 1908, offers a tantalizing array. ◈ *C/Portaferrissa 8 • Map L3*

7 Cereria Subirà
Founded in 1761, this is Barcelona's oldest shop. Today you'll find it crammed with every kind of candle imaginable. ◈ *Baixada Llibreteria 7 • Map N4*

8 L'Arca de l'Àvia
Amazing antique clothing from flapper dresses to boned corsets, silk shawls, puff sleeved shirts and pin-tucked shirt fronts. There's also a selection of antique dolls and fans. ◈ *C/Banys Nous 20 • Map M3*

9 Guantería Alonso
This long-established shop is still the place to visit if you are looking for colourful hand-painted fans, handmade gloves, delicately embroidered shawls, ornamental combs and other traditional Spanish accessories. ◈ *C/Santa Anna 27 • Map M2*

10 Vila Viniteca
One of the city's best wine merchants stocking wines and spirits. An adjoining shop sells top quality Spanish delicacies, including hams, cheeses and olive oil. ◈ *C/Agullers 7*

For tips on shopping and standard opening hours **See p139**

75

Left **La Vinya del Senyor** Right **Schilling**

Cocktail & Conversation Spots

1 Schilling
Fronted by large windows overlooking the throngs on Carrer Ferran, this spacious bar draws a sociable mix of both visitors and locals. ✆ C/Ferran 23 • Map M4

2 Bar L'Ascensor
An old-fashioned, dark-wood *ascensor* (elevator) serves as the entrance to this dimly lit, convivial bar frequented by a cocktail-swilling crowd. ✆ C/Bellafila 3 • Map M4

3 Café del Born Nou
This café is located opposite the Mercat del Born, and offers coffee and cakes, as well as a range of salads, sandwiches and light meals. It attracts a relaxed, arty crowd, who linger over their newspapers with a coffee.
✆ Plaça Comercial 10

4 Ginger
An elegant bar that serves fine wines, champagne, cava, cocktails and a variety of original tapas to a glamorous crowd.
✆ Palma de Sant Just 1 • Map N4
• Closed Sun, Mon

5 Glaciar
Occupying a prime corner of Plaça Reial, this atmospheric café-bar brings in all types. Grab a spot on the terrace with a front-row view of the *plaça* activities.
✆ Pl Reial 3 • Map L4

6 Milk
Decorated like a luxurious living room, with elegant sofas, gold picture frames, chandeliers and 1950s wallpaper, Milk serves brunch (from 10am to 4pm), lunch and dinner daily.
✆ C/Gignàs 21 • Map M5

7 La Vinya del Senyor
A classy, yet cosy, bar attracting wine lovers from all over the city, who come to sample a rich array of Spanish and international varieties.
✆ Pl Santa Maria 5 • Map N5

8 El Pilé 43
This hip little bar is packed with funky 1960s and 1970s retro furniture, all of which is for sale. Sink into a sofa, sip a mojito and ponder which items could be squeezed into a suitcase. ✆ C/Aglà 4 • Map L4

9 Juanra Falces
The original cocktail bar in El Born, the intimate, 1950s-style Juanra Falces pours nice (read: potent) cocktails for locals. ✆ C/Rec 24 • Map P4 • Closed Sun & Mon

10 Mudanzas
This long-time favourite hang-out has circular marble tables, black-and-white tiled floors and an informal, "everybody's welcome" vibe. ✆ C/Vidrieria 15 • Map P5

Left **Sidecar Factory Club** Right **Jamboree**

🔟 Clubs & Music Venues

1 Jamboree
This Barri Gòtic institution has live jazz every night (11pm–1am). It then evolves into a dance club, with DJs spinning everything from hip-hop to R&B and salsa. ✆ *Pl Reial 17 • Map L4 • Adm*

2 Sala Monasterio
This small and atmospheric basement bar has a little stage for live gigs. World music, jazz and blues are most popular, but the eclectic programme features most kinds of music. ✆ *Passeig Isabel II No. 4*

3 Polaroids
A fabulously kitsch bar, with 80s-style decor and great retro sounds. Drinks are well priced and usually come with big bowls of free popcorn. Be sure to get here early – the place is always packed. ✆ *C/Còdols 29 • Map M5*

4 Harlem Jazz Club
Dark and smoky, this kickback jazz haunt features a choice line-up of jazz and blues, flamenco fusion, reggae and African music. ✆ *Comtessa de Sobradiel 8 • Map M5 • Usually free • Closed Mon, concerts from 9pm*

5 Fantàstico Club
Pop, electro pop, and candy-coloured decor make this club a hit. ✆ *Passatge Escudellers 3 • Map L5*

6 Karma
The hippie origins and 1970s glamour at this club are as popular as ever. ✆ *Pl Reial 10 • Map L4 • Adm • Closed Mon*

7 Magic
Live music is played at this rock club at weekends by new, up-and-coming Spanish bands. After the show, the dancing goes on until 5:30am. ✆ *Pg Picasso 40 • Map P4 • Adm • Closed Sun–Wed*

8 Café Royale
Next to the Plaça Reial, this club has minimalist, elegant décor and a small dance floor. There are occasional live music and flamenco concerts. ✆ *C/Nou de Zurbano 3 • Map L5 • Closed Sun & Mon*

9 Marula Café
An intimate club featuring local and international DJs and upbeat live music every day of the week. ✆ *C/Escudellers 49 • Map L5 • DA*

🔟 Sidecar Factory Club
Barcelona's music scene is like a motorbike to which Sidecar is inseparably bound. They say the American 6th fleet once hired the whole venue and made merry. There's music, cabaret and good food. ✆ *Pl Reial 7 • Map L4 • Adm • Closed Sun*

For Barcelona's best nightlife **See pp46–7**

Left **Terrace, Cafè-Bar L'Antiquari** Centre **Ice cream, Cafè d'Estiu** Right **Caelum**

🔟 Cafés & Light Eats

Cafè d'Estiu
1 This terrace café on the patio of the Museu Frederic Marès *(see p72)* is replete with stone pillars, climbing ivy and orange trees. Your museum ticket entitles you to a discount. ◈ *Pl de Sant Iu 5–6* • *Map N3* • *Closed Mon & Oct–Mar* • *DA*

La Báscula
2 This quirky café, set in an old chocolate factory, has several vegetarian dishes and a range of tasty cakes. ◈ *C/Flassaders 30* • *Map P4* • *Closed Mon & Tue* • *93 319 98 66*

Cafè-Bar L'Antiquari
3 In summer, bask in the old town's medieval atmosphere at the Plaça del Rei terrace. By night, sip Rioja in the intimate, rustic basement bodega.
◈ *C/Veguer 13* • *Map N4*

La Granja
4 This delightful little café in the Gothic Quarter is ideal for a break from sightseeing or shopping. Admire the Roman stone wall while enjoying coffee and pastries, or a selection of light snacks. ◈ *C/Banys Nous 4* • *Map M3*

Tetería Salterio
5 Sit back and relax with tea and sweet Arab cakes. Do not miss the Sado, an Oriental style pizza with a variety of fillings.
◈ *C/Sant Domenec del Call 4* • *Map M4*

Café Bliss
6 Take a break from exploring the Gothic Quarter at this friendly café. It serves divine cakes, light meals and snacks. Ask for a table outside. ◈ *Plaça Sant Just* • *Map N4* • *93 268 10 22*

Drac Café
7 The best option for a coffee in the Parc de la Ciutadella is this charming outdoor café. Serves salads and sandwiches. ◈ *Parc de la Ciutadella* • *Map Q4* • *Closed Dec–Feb*

Caelum
8 Upstairs sells honey, preserves and other foods made in convents and monasteries all over Spain. Downstairs you can sample all the delicacies in a café on the site of 15th-century baths. ◈ *C/Palla 8* • *Map M3*

Bar del Pla
9 An interesting combination of Spanish tapas with a French twist. Try the pig's trotters with *foie gras* or the squid ink croquettes. ◈ *C/Montcada 2* • *Map P4* • *Closed Mon*

La Granja Pallaresa
10 This family-run *xocolateria* has long been serving up thick hot chocolate and *xurros* (fried dough strips) for dunking. ◈ *C/Petritxol 11* • *Map L3* • *Closed from 1–4pm daily*

For more cafés in the Barri Gòtic **See pp42–3**

Price Categories

For a three-course meal for one with half a bottle of wine (or equivalent meal), taxes and extra charges.

€	under €15
€€	€15–25
€€€	€25–35
€€€€	€35–45
€€€€€	over €45

Cal Pep

🏅10 Restaurants & Tapas Bars

1 Bar Mundial
Opened in 1925 and still boasting the original marble tables, this classic tapas bar is one of the best. The menu changes constantly. ◈ *Plaça de Sant Agustí Vell 1 • Map P3 • 93 319 90 56 • Closed 2 weeks in Aug • €€€*

2 Cal Pep
Taste delicious tapas, including the finest seafood, at this established eatery. ◈ *Pl de les Olles 8 • Map P5 • 93 310 79 61 • Closed Sat dinner, Sun, Mon lunch, Aug • €€€*

3 Cafè de l'Acadèmia
Superb Catalan cuisine and top-notch desserts are served at this restaurant in an 18th-century building. ◈ *C/Lledó 1 • Map N4 • 93 315 00 26 • Closed Sat, Sun, Aug • €€€€*

4 Comerç 24
The highlight of this innovative restaurant is the constantly changing menu. Each *platillo* (little plate) blends unique flavours to create an exquisite dish. ◈ *C/Comerç 24 • Map P4 • 93 319 21 02 • Closed Sun & Mon • DA • €€€€€*

5 Senyor Parellada
Excellent Catalan cuisine, including speciality *bacalao* (cod) and *butifarra* (sausage), is the deal at this restaurant. ◈ *C/Argentería 37 • Map N4 • 93 310 50 94 • DA • €€€*

6 Agut
For over 75 years, this friendly, family restaurant has been delighting patrons with excellent Catalan cuisine at decent prices. ◈ *C/Gignàs 16 • Map M5 • 93 315 17 09 • Closed Sun eve & Mon, 1 week in Jan, Aug • DA • €€€€*

7 Bodega La Palma
This Bohemian restaurant in a former wine cellar offers tapas such as stuffed Piquillo peppers. ◈ *Palma de Sant Just 7 • Map M4 • 93 315 06 56 • Closed Sun, 2 weeks in Aug • €€*

8 Big Fish
Stylish but relaxed, with comfy sofas, Big Fish serves seafood and a range of sushi. The music cranks up late in the evening, when the restaurant morphs into a bar. ◈ *C/Comercial 9 • Map Q4 • 93 268 17 28 • Closed Mon • €€€€*

9 El Xampanyet
An old-fashioned bar popular for the fizzy *cava* and range of simple tapas. ◈ *C/Montcada 22 • Map P4 • 93 319 70 03 • Closed Sun eve, & Mon • €€*

10 Govinda
This soothing eatery offers vegetarian Indian main dishes and delectable desserts, but no alcohol. ◈ *Pl Vila de Madrid 4 • Map M2 • 93 318 77 29 • Closed Sun eve & Mon eve • DA • €€*

Unless otherwise stated, all restaurants accept credit cards.
For tips on dining and standard opening hours **See p138**

79

Left **Plaça de Joan Coromines** Right **Columns, Església de Sant Pau del Camp**

El Raval

THE SLEEK, SHINY, WHITE WALLS *of the Museu d'Art Contemporani (MACBA) juxtapose the decrepit, ramshackle tenement buildings; Asian grocery stores sell herbs and spices next to what were once the most decadent brothels in Europe; and smoky, decades-old bars share dark, narrow streets with high-ceilinged art galleries showcasing video installations. The old-town barri of El Raval is a traditional working-class neighbourhood in flux. Since the 1990s it has been undergoing an enthusiastic urban renewal, led by the arrival of the MACBA. The barri now even has its very own Rambla, a pedestrian street called La Rambla del Raval. Not surprisingly, all of this has sparked a real-estate boom, with renovated old-fashioned flats now commanding top-tier prices and acting as a magnet to the city's young, savvy crowd.*

Stained-glass window,
Museu Marítim

🔟 Sights

1. Museu d'Art Contemporani (MACBA)
2. Centre de Cultura Con-temporània & Foment de les Arts Decoratives
3. Museu Marítim
4. Palau Güell
5. La Rambla del Raval
6. Carrer Nou de la Rambla
7. Carrers Tallers & Riera Baixa
8. Barri Xinès
9. Antic Hospital de la Santa Creu
10. Església de Sant Pau del Camp

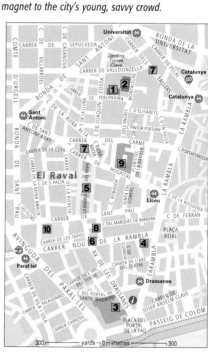

For sights & attractions on La Rambla **See pp12–13**

1 Museu d'Art Contemporani (MACBA)

An eclectic array of work by big-name Spanish and international contemporary artists is gathered in the city's contemporary art museum. Excellent temporary exhibitions feature everything from mixed media to sculpture and photography. *See pp28–9.*

2 Centre de Cultura Contemporània (CCCB) & Foment de les Arts Decoratives

Housed in the 18th-century Casa de la Caritat, the CCCB is a focal point for the city's thriving contemporary arts scene. It hosts innovative art exhibitions, lectures, film screenings and more, including multimedia and technology fairs during the popular Festival del Sònar *(see p65)*. A medieval courtyard is dazzlingly offset by a massive, angled glass wall, which has been cunningly designed to reflect the city's skyline. Nearby, Foment de les Arts Decoratives *(see p84)* is an umbrella organization of art and design groups, founded in 1903 and housed in the restored, Gothic-style, 16th-century Convent dels Àngels. Here you'll find exhibits, lectures and debates (open Mon–Fri). *See pp28–9.*

3 Museu Marítim

Barcelona's mighty seafaring legacy comes to life at this museum housed in the vast 13th-century Drassanes Reials (Royal Shipyards).

Central salon cupola, Palau Güell

After a major renovation, the museum will reopen in late 2014 with brand-new displays and high-tech design. Meanwhile, it is possible to admire temporary exhibitions under the spectacular Gothic arches where the royal galleys were once constructed. It is also possible to visit the Pailebot *Santa Eulàlia (see p98),* a restored wooden sailing ship from 1918. ◈ *Av de les Drassanes • Map K6 • Closed until late 2014; temporary exhibitions open 10am–8pm daily • Adm • www.mmb.cat*

4 Palau Güell

For an artist, a wealthy patron spells survival. The luck of young Gaudí turned when count Eusebi Güell recognized his talents. In 1886, Güell commissioned Gaudí to build a mansion that would set the count apart from his wealthy neighbours. The result is the Palau Güell, one of Gaudí's earliest works. An imposing façade gives way to an interior of lavish pillars and wooden ceilings, while the rooftop has mosaic chimneys. ◈ *C/Nou de la Rambla 3–5 • Map L4 • Open 10am–8pm daily (to 5:30pm Nov–Mar); last adm: 1 hr before closing • Adm • www.palauguell.cat*

Puzzle table, Museu d'Art Contemporani

For more on Antoni Gaudí **See p11**

La Rambla del Raval

5 This palm tree-lined, pedestrian walkway started as an attempt by city planners to spark a similar social environment to that of the city's famed La Rambla *(see pp12–13)*. The striking, conical Barceló Hotel, with its panoramic rooftop terrace, and the sleek Filmoteca, a film archive complete with café and bookshop, are signs of the area's unstoppable gentrification. New shops, bars and cafés mean the Rambla del Raval could well rival its cousin in years to come. ◈ *Map K4*

Carrer Nou de la Rambla

6 In the first half of the 19th century, El Raval's main street was a notorious strip of cabarets, brothels and other nocturnal dens. Today it still bustles with transactions, but of a different sort. Frayed-at-the-edge local eateries, ethnic grocery stores, and discount clothing and shoe shops dot the street. And nightspots, such as the atmospheric London Bar *(see p86)*, which have kept their age-old identity and fixtures, lure partying visitors. ◈ *Map J5*

Carrers Tallers & Riera Baixa

7 Looking for bootleg CDs of Madonna's European tour? Or vintage blue-and-white French navy tops once favoured by the

Shoppers, Carrer Tallers

likes of Picasso? Dotting Carrers Tallers and Riera Baixa, in the heart of El Raval, are many vintage music and clothing shops selling everything from vinyl to the latest CDs, original Hawaiian shirts and Dickies workwear. On Saturdays, Carrer Riera Baixa has its own market (11am–9pm), with the stores displaying their wares on the street. ◈ *Map L1 & K3*

Barri Xinès

8 The first thing locals will say when you ask about the Barri Xinès is that it no longer exists; the second is that the name has no real connection with the Chinese *(Xinès)*. Both statements are true. This *barri*, unfolding south from Carrer Sant Pau towards Drassanes, was once one of Europe's most infamous neighbourhoods, inhabited by the poor and working-class and rife with prostitutes, pimps and drug dealers. Today, due to enthusiastic clean-up efforts, mere vestiges remain of the *barri*'s previous life (though some alleys still hint at illicit activity). As

Record shop, Carrer Tallers

for the name, the area has nothing to do with the Chinese, but was named in the *barri*'s early-1900s heyday as a general reference to its large immigrant population. Today you can browse in cheap thrift shops and small grocery stores by day and bar-hop by night. ◈ *Map K4*

9 Antic Hospital de la Santa Creu

This Gothic hospital complex (1401), now home to the National Library and various cultural organizations, is a reminder of the neighbourhood's medieval past. Within, you can wander a pleasant garden surrounded by Gothic pillars; a reader's card is necessary for admission to the library. ◈ *Entrances on C/Carme & C/Hospital 56 • Map K3 • Courtyard open 9am–8pm daily • Free*

Cloister, Església de Sant Pau del Camp

10 Església de Sant Pau del Camp

Deep in the heart of El Raval is this Romanesque church, one of the oldest in Barcelona. Originally founded as a Benedictine monastery in the 9th century and subsequently rebuilt, this ancient church reveals a 12th-century cloister. ◈ *C/Sant Pau 101 • Map J4 • Open 10am–1:30pm, 4–7:30pm Mon–Sat. Mass 8pm Sat, noon Sun • Adm*

A Ramble in El Raval

Morning

🕐 Start your ramble mid-morning by perusing the innovative temporary art exhibits at the **CCCB** *(see p81)*. Here the two world's have meshed harmoniously. The eye-catching blend of old-meets-new in this cutting-edge art space provides a fitting introduction to El Raval's new identity. Head south along C/Montalegre to the Plaça dels Àngels.

🏛 On the square, watching the skateboarders in front of the **MACBA** *(see p81)*, then pop into the **Foment de les Arts Decoratives** *(see p81)*, which features art and design exhibitions. Round off your art amble with a trip down nearby C/Doctor Dou, which is speckled with commercial art galleries. If you're looking for unique items to jazz up your home, pop into **Transforma** *(see p84)*.

Afternoon

From here, it's a short saunter to **Mercat de La Boqueria** *(see p12)*. Walk along C/Carme, turn left onto C/Jerusalem, and go into the back entrance of this cavernous market. Make a beeline for El Quim de La Boqueria 🍴 (stall 584–585) where you can pull up a stool and dig into fresh fare from baby prawns drizzled in olive oil and garlic to steamed mussels. After, head to the medieval gardens of the **Antic Hospital de la Santa Creu**, off C/Hospital, and take in the Gothic ambience of pillared arcades and courtyards. Then, get to **Marsella** 🍸 *(see p86)* and kick-start the evening with an absinthe before making for **London Bar** *(see p86)* with its *Modernista* decor.

Left **Galeria dels Àngels** Right **Window, Foment de les Arts Decoratives**

Galleries & Design Shops

Galeria dels Àngels
Emerging and established contemporary artists from home and abroad are shown at this cutting-edge photography, painting and sculpture gallery. ⊗ *C/Pintor Fortuny, 27 • Map L2 • Closed Sat & Sun*

Transforma
This store on one of the most arty streets in El Raval stocks an innovative range of lamps, furnishings, ceramics and handmade jewellery. It is a good place to find unusual gifts. ⊗ *C/Doctor Dou 16 • Map L2 • 93 301 89 05 • Closed Sun*

Siesta
Part boutique, part art gallery, this shop offers unique ceramics, jewellery and glass art, as well as hosting temporary exhibitions. ⊗ *C/Ferlandina 18 • Map K2 • 93 317 80 41 • Closed Sat pm & Sun*

Nogueras Blanchard
Daring, contemporary international art is on show at this prestigious gallery. ⊗ *C/Xuclà 7 • Map L2 • 93 342 57 21 • Closed Sat & Sun*

Tinta Invisible
This workshop and exhibition is dedicated to "artists of the book". On show are engravings, bookbinding, prints and graphic design. ⊗ *C/ Lleó 6 • Map K1 • 93 301 29 42 • Closed Sat & Sun*

La Capella
This Gothic chapel is now a contemporary art gallery, run by the city and dedicated to emerging artists. ⊗ *C/Hospital 56 • Map K3 • Open noon–2pm & 4–8pm Tue–Sat, 11am–2pm Sun*

Foment de les Arts Decoratives (FAD)
Check out the ongoing exhibitions hosted by FAD, a century-old arts, crafts and design organization. ⊗ *Pl Àngels 5–6 • Map K2 • Closed Sun*

La Xina A.R.T.
The very latest on the contemporary art scene features at this innovative gallery, started by four local artists in the late 1990s. ⊗ *Hort de la Bomba 6 • Map J4 • Open 5:30–8:30pm Wed–Sat*

Loring Art
Multimedia and digital design are spotlighted at this trendy bookshop space. ⊗ *C/Gravina 8 • Map L1 • Closed Sat & Sun*

The Air Shop
A range of fun inflatable products by young designers are for sale and on display here: flower vases and accessories to furniture and all kinds of personalised items. ⊗ *C/Àngels 20 • Map K2 • Closed Sun & Mon am*

Art aficionados gather at galleries for openings once a month (Tue–Thu). Enquire at individual galleries for more information.

Left **Holala** Right **Shop window, Revólver Records**

🔟 Vintage & Second-Hand Shops

1 Lullaby
Designer labels, beautiful accessories and even some quirky *objets d'art* – you'll find them all here. Prices are reasonable. ◈ C/Riera Baixa 22 • Map K3

2 Holala
Rummage for an outfit at this three-floor vintage store, with everything from original silk kimonos to army pants and colourful 1950s bathing suits. ◈ C/Tallers 73 • Map L1

3 Galalith
This tiny, magical shop specializes in vintage-inspired accessories. All pendants, scarves, purses and bags have a delightfully retro feel. ◈ C/Riera Baixa 5 • Map K3

4 Lailo
In this theatre-turned-vintage store, you'll find everything from glitzy 1950s cocktail dresses to 1920s costumes. ◈ C/Riera Baixa 20 • Map K3

5 Revólver Records
The speciality here is classic rock – as shown by the wall art depicting The Rolling Stones and Jimi Hendrix. One floor houses CDs, the other a huge selection of vinyl. ◈ C/Tallers 13 • Map L2 • Closed Sun

6 Wilde Vintage
This dimly lit, boudoiresque boutique is lined with vintage sunglasses in every shape and colour, from aviator shades to a pair of cat's-eyes specs from the 1960s. ◈ C/Joaquin Costa 2 • Map K2

7 Holala Plaza
This huge shop in the heart of the Raval sells second hand clothes, furniture and bric-a-brac, attracting a trendy crowd. The adjoining gallery houses ever-changing exhibitions. ◈ Plaça Castella 2 • Map L1 • Closed Sun

8 Ulleres M Assumpta
This tiny shop sells vintage artisan glasses and sunglasses, along with its own designs. ◈ C/Ramalleres 3 • Map L2 • Closed Sat pm & Sun

9 Discos Tesla
This tiny, but well-stocked, record and CD store focuses on alternative music from decades past. It is the kind of place where you can hum a few lines of a song and the owner will track it down. ◈ C/Tallers 3 • Map L2

10 GI Joe Surplus
One of Spain's few army and navy surplus stores, where you can find bags, backpacks and clothing from the Russian, Israeli and US militaries. ◈ Ronda Sant Antoni 49 • Map K1

Left **Zelig** Right **Zentraus**

Bars & Clubs

1 Bar Almirall
The *Modernista* doors swing open to a young, friendly crowd at Barcelona's oldest watering hole. Founded in 1860, the bar has many original fittings, plus eclectic music and strong cocktails. ✆ *C/Joaquin Costa 33 • Map K2*

2 Zelig
Intimate and welcoming, this gay-friendly cocktail bar is a great place to start the night. There are excellent cocktails – including a mean mojito – and light snacks. ✆ *C/Carme 116 • Map K2 • Closed Mon*

3 Bar Resolis
Formerly an old-fashioned neighbourhood bar, this is now an appealing boho-chic tavern with a small terrace. Wine and cocktails accompany delicious tapas. ✆ *C/Riera Baixa 22 • Map K3*

4 Marsella
This dimly lit *Modernista* bar serves up cocktails and absinthe to long-time regulars and first-timers. ✆ *C/Sant Pau 65 • Map K4*

5 Zentraus
One of the most stylish bars in the area, Zentraus has a trendy red-black-and-white decor and cool lighting. A restaurant until 1am, the tables are cleared once the DJ starts. ✆ *Rambla de Raval 41 • Map K4 • Closed Mon*

6 Betty Ford's
A laidback cocktail bar on lively Carrer Joaquin Costa, Betty Ford's has a soothing chill-out vibe. ✆ *Carrer Joaquin Costa 56 • Map K1*

7 Moog
Big-name DJs spin techno and electronica, but for a boogie to classic 1980s hits head for the second floor. ✆ *C/Arc del Teatre 3 • Map L5 • Adm*

8 Boadas Cocktail Bar
This smooth little cocktail bar, founded in 1933, continues to mix the meanest martinis in town for an elbow-to-elbow crowd. ✆ *C/Tallers 1 • Map L2 • Closed Sun*

9 London Bar
This cluttered bar has long been *de rigueur*, once with the likes of Picasso, Hemingway and Miró. Sip cocktails and enjoy the original *Modernista* furnishings. ✆ *C/Nou de la Rambla 34 • Map K4 • Closed Mon*

10 La Penúltima
A small, quirky bar featuring a collection of Barbie and Ken dolls in unusual positions. It's a gay-friendly spot, and is perfect for the first drink of the night. Alternative music is predominantly played. ✆ *C/Riera Alta 40 • Map J2*

For Barcelona's best nightlife **See pp46–7**

Price Categories

For a three-course meal for one with half a bottle of wine (or equivalent meal), taxes and extra charges.	**€** under €15
	€€ €15–25
	€€€ €25–35
	€€€€ €35–45
	€€€€€ over €45

Ca L'Isidre

TOP 10 Good-Value Eats

1 Biblioteca
The walls at this elegant restaurant are lined with antique books. Food is made using fresh market ingredients, and you can see the cooks work in the open kitchen. Book ahead. ◈ *C/Junta de Comerç 28 • Map K4 • 93 412 62 21 • Closed Mon lunch, Sun • DA • €€€€*

2 Ànima
A sleek restaurant serving sophisticated Mediterranean cuisine. Great value lunch menu (€10). ◈ *C/Àngels 6 • Map K2 • 93 342 49 12 • Closed Sun & lunch in Aug • €€€*

3 Ca L'Isidre
Picasso, Tapiès and even Woody Allen have dined on Catalan fare at this artists' hang-out. ◈ *C/Les Flors 12 • Map J4 • 93 441 11 39 • Closed Sat (in summer), Sun, Easter, Aug, Christmas • DA • €€€€€*

4 Teresa Carles
Come here for imaginative vegetarian fare, such as *crêpes* with artichokes and brie. The set lunch menu is great value (€9.50, Mon–Fri). ◈ *C/Jovellanos 2 • Map L1 • 93 317 18 29 • €€*

5 Olivia Café
A quiet, modern café with Scandinavian design, Olivia serves good coffee and some of the best cakes in town. ◈ *C/Pintor Fortuny 22 • Map L2 • 93 318 63 80 • Closed Mon • €*

6 El Jardí
Located in one of the prettiest spots in the city (the courtyard of the Antic Hospital de la Santa Creu), El Jardí serves delicious soups, salads and *crêpes*. ◈ *C/Hospital 56 • Map K3 • Closed Mon • €*

7 Bacaro
Tucked behind the Boquería market, this convivial little Italian bar/restaurant serves a changing menu of modern Venetian cuisine. ◈ *C/Jerusalén 6 • Map L3 • Closed Sun • 695 796 066 • €€€*

8 Marmalade
A loft-style bar providing snacks and light meals in the evenings (fajitas, fish and chips, stir fries), as well as cocktails. Marmalade also serves a great brunch at weekends. ◈ *C/Riera Alta 4–6 • Map J2 • 93 442 39 66 • €*

9 Pla dels Àngels
With a lively terrace and a cosy interior, this is a great spot for salads, pastas and Mediterranean-Oriental fusion dishes. ◈ *C/Ferladina 23 • Map K2 • DA • €€*

10 L'Havana
Despite the name, this eatery serves superb Catalan cuisine. Try classic dishes such as pigs' trotters, or the fresh fish of the day. ◈ *C/Lleó 1 • Map K2 • 93 302 21 06 • Closed Sun eve, Mon • €€*

For tips on dining and standard opening hours **See p138**

Left **Palau Nacional** Right **Estadi Olímpic**

Montjuïc

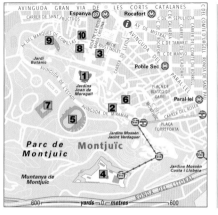

NAMED THE "JEWISH MOUNTAIN", *after an important Jewish cemetery that existed here in the Middle Ages, this sizeable and mountainous park rises 213 m (700 ft) above the port. The park itself was first landscaped for the 1929 International Exhibition, when the elegant Palau Nacional and the strikingly modern Mies van der Rohe Pavilion were also built. During the following decade, the area fell into general disuse and soon became synonymous with decline. Together with the grim shadow cast over the hill by the castle, which for years acted as a slaughterhouse for Franco's firing squads, it is little short of miraculous that Montjuïc is now one of Barcelona's biggest tourist draws. However, as the main site for the 1992 Olympics, held on its southern slopes, Montjuïc was given a comprehensive face-lift and the area was transformed into a beautiful green oasis, with two fabulous art museums and a host of stunning sports facilities.*

Statue, Castell de Montjuïc

All these elements are interconnected by a network of exterior escalators and interlaced with quiet, shady gardens, which offer dazzling views over Barcelona and a welcome respite from the bustle of the city.

Sights

1. Palau Nacional & Museu Nacional d'Art de Catalunya
2. Fundació Joan Miró
3. Font Màgica
4. Castell de Montjuïc
5. Estadi Olímpic
6. Teatre Grec
7. Palau Sant Jordi
8. Pavelló Mies van der Rohe
9. Poble Espanyol
10. CaixaForum

For more on Barcelona's history See pp30–31

Fountains, Palau Nacional

Palau Nacional & Museu Nacional d'Art de Catalunya

The Palau Nacional is home to the Museu Nacional d'Art de Catalunya which exhibits Catalonia's historic art collections. Boasting one of Europe's finest displays of Romanesque art, the museum includes a series of 12th-century frescoes, rescued from Catalan Pyrenean churches and painstakingly reassembled in a series of galleries here. See pp18–19.

Fundació Joan Miró

One of Catalonia's most representative painters, Joan Miró (1893–1983), donated many of the 11,000 works held by the museum. Housed in a stark, white building designed by his friend, architect Josep Lluís Sert, the collection is the world's most complete array of Miro's work. See pp22–3.

Font Màgica

Below the cascades and fountains that decend from the Palau Nacional is the Magic Fountain, designed by Carles Buigas for the International Exhibition of 1929. As darkness descends, countless jets of water are choreographed in a mesmerizing sound and light show. When the water meets in a single jet it can soar to 15m (50ft). The extravagant finale is often accompanied by a recording of Freddie Mercury and Montserrat Caballé singing the anthem *Barcelona* as the fountain fades from pink to green and back to white before silently and gracefully disappearing. The Four Columns behind the fountain represent the Cataln flag and are a symbol of the Catalanism movement. ⊗ *Av de la Reina Maria Cristina • Map B4 • May–Sep: every 30 minutes 9–11:30pm Thu–Sun (last show at 11pm); Oct–Apr: every 30 minutes 7–9pm Fri & Sat (last show at 8:30pm) • Free • DA*

Castell de Montjuïc

Castell de Montjuïc

Dominating Montjuïc's hill, this gloomy castle was once a prison and torture centre for political prisoners. At the end of the Spanish Civil War, 4,000 Catalan nationalists and republicans were shot in the nearby Fossar de la Pedrera, now a grassy field overlooked by thick stone walls. After such a tragic history, the castle is entering a happier phase: it has been developed into an international peace centre, but visitors can still climb the sturdy bastions for superb views of the port below. ⊗ *C/Castell • Map B6 • Open daily • Free*

The funicular connects Metro Paral·lel with the Fundació Joan Miró and the cable cars that continue up to the Castell de Montjuïc.

89

Estadi Olímpic

5 The stadium was first built for the 1936 Workers' Olympics, which were cancelled with the outbreak of the Spanish Civil War *(see p31)*. The original Neo-Classical façade is still in place, but the stadium was rebuilt for the 1992 Olympic Games *(see p31)*. It is home to Espanyol football team *(see p61)*. The interactive Museu Olímpic i de l'Esport, nearby, is dedicated to all aspects of sport. ◈ *Av de l'Estadi 60 • Map B5 • Museum: open 10am–6pm (to 8pm Apr–Sep) Tue–Sat, 10am–2:30pm Sun. Stadium not open to visitors • Adm • DA*

Teatre Grec

6 This beautiful, open-air amphitheatre *(see p66)* was inspired by the Classical ideas of what was known as *Noucentisme*. This late 19th-century architectural movement was a reaction to the overly decorative nature of *Modernisme*. With its leafy, green backdrop and beautiful gardens, there are few places more enchanting than this to watch *Swan Lake* or listen to some jazz. The theatre is used for shows during the summertime Grec Festival *(see p65)*, when it also becomes home to a luxurious outdoor restaurant. ◈ *Pg Santa Madrona • Map C4 • 10am–dusk • Free (when there are no shows)*

Palau Sant Jordi

7 The star of all the Olympic installations is this steel-and-glass indoor stadium *(see p66)* designed by Japanese architect Arata Isozaki. Holding around 17,000 people, the stadium is the home of the city's basketball team *(see p61)*. The esplanade – a surreal forest of concrete and metal pillars – was designed by Aiko Isozaki, Arata's wife. Further down the hill are the indoor and outdoor Bernat Picornell Olympic pools *(see p60)*; which are open to the public. ◈ *Passeig Olímpic 5–7 • Map A4 • Open 10am–6pm (to 8pm May–Sep) Sat & Sun • Free • DA*

Palau Sant Jordi

Pavelló Mies van der Rohe

8 You might wonder exactly what this box-like pavilion of stone, marble, onyx and glass is doing bang in the middle of Montjuïc's monumental architecture. Years ahead of its time, this surprisingly rationalist gem represents Germany's contribution to the 1929 Exhibition. Built by Ludwig Mies van der Rohe (1886–1969), the elegant pavilion was soon demolished, only to be reconstructed in 1986. Inside, the elegant sculpture *Morning* by Georg Kolbe (1877–1947) is reflected

Barcelona Chairs, Pavelló Mies van der Rohe

 You can board the Montjuïc Bus Turístic (see p133), which ferries visitors up the hill from Plaça d'Espanya and back (April to October).

Poble Espanyol

A Day in Montjuïc

Morning

To get to the **Fundació Joan Miró** (see pp22–3) before the crowds and with energy to spare, hop on the funicular from Paral·lel metro station. From here it is a short walk to the museum, where you'll need an hour and a half to absorb the impressive collection of Miró paintings, sketches and sculptures. When you've had your fill of contemporary art, refuel with a *cafè amb llet* (see p43) on the restaurant terrace before backtracking along Av de Miramar and jumping on the cable car up to **Castell de Montjuïc** (see p89). Wander the castle gardens and look out over the city and the bustling docks. Return to Av de Miramar by cable car and follow the signs to the **Palau Nacional** (see p89), where you can lunch on typical Catalan cuisine with a modern twist in the elegant Oleum (see p95).

Afternoon

Afterwards, spend an hour perusing the **MNAC**'s (see pp18–19) extraordinary Romanesque art collection. When you exit, turn right and then follow the signs to the Olympic complex. The **Estadi Olímpic** is worth a look, but the silver-domed **Palau Sant Jordi** steals the limelight. Nearby, at Bernat Picornell, spend the late afternoon cooling down with a dip in the fantastic open-air pool. If it's summer, there may even be a film showing. From here it is just a short stroll to the **Poble Espanyol** where you can settle in at a terrace bar in Plaça de Mayor and sip a *cuba libre* as night descends.

n a small lake. ✪ *Av Francesc Ferrer i Guàrdia 7* • *Map B4* • *Open 10am–8pm daily* • *Adm*

Poble Espanyol

This Spanish *poble* (village) has been recreated from a hotchpotch of scaled-down famous buildings and streets from around Spain. Although a bit tacky, it has become a centre for arts and crafts, including an impressive glass-blowers' workshop. There are restaurants and cafés aplenty, and a couple of trendy nightclubs (see p95). ✪ *Av Francesc Ferrer i Guàrdia* • *Map A3* • *Open 9am–8pm Mon, 9am–2am Tue–Thu, 9am–4am Fri, 9am–5pm Sat, 9am–midnight Sun* • *Adm*

CaixaForum

The Fundació La Caixa's impressive collection of contemporary art is housed in a former textile factory, designed by *Modernista* architect Puig i Cadafalch. The collection assembles some 800 works by Spanish and foreign artists, shown in rotation along with temporary international exhibitions. ✪ *Av Francesc Ferrer i Guàrdia 6–8* • *Map B3* • *Open 10am–8pm daily (to 9pm Sat & Sun, to 11pm on Wed in Jul & Aug)* • *Free* • *DA*

Following pages **13th-century altar frontal, Museu Nacional d'Art de Catalunya**

Left **Jardins Mossèn Cinto Verdaguer** Right **Jardins del Castell**

Parks & Gardens

Jardins Mossèn Costa i Llobera
These are among Europe's most important cactus gardens. They are particularly impressive as the sun sets, when surreal and shapes and shadows emerge. ◈ Map C5

Jardí Botànic
These wild gardens offer splendid vistas and hundreds of examples of typical Mediterranean vegetation. ◈ Map A4 • Open Feb, Mar, Oct: 10am–6pm daily; Apr, May, Sep: 10am–7pm daily; Jun–Aug: 10am–8pm daily; Nov–Jan: 10am–5pm daily • Adm; free last Sun of month & every Sun from 3pm

Jardins Mossèn Cinto Verdaguer
The best time to visit these wonderfully elegant gardens is in spring when the plants are in blossom and the colours and aromas are in full force. ◈ Map C5

Jardins del Castell
Cannons among the rose bushes, and pathways along the walls of a flower-filled moat, are the highlights of these gardens, which ring the castle. ◈ Map B5

Jardins del Teatre Grec
Reminiscent of the Hanging Gardens of Babylon, this gracious oasis surrounding the Greek amphitheatre is officially known as La Rosadela. ◈ Map C4

Jardins de Miramar
Opposite the Miramar, these gardens are scattered with stairways leading to enchanting leafy groves with vistas. ◈ Map C5

Jardins Laribal
This multi-level park hides a small *Modernista* house, by Puig i Cadafalch, and the Font del Gat – a drinking fountain, which has inspired many local songs. ◈ Map B4

Jardins de Joan Maragall
An avenue lined with sculptures by Frederic Marès and Ernest Maragall is the main delight here. The garden also has the last of the city's *ginjoler* trees. ◈ Map B4 • Open 10am–3pm Sat & Sun

Muntanya de Montjuïc
A multitude of secret paths leads through wild gardens on Montjuïc's south side, the only part of the mountain that remains untamed. ◈ Map A5

El Mirador del Llobregat
A viewing area with small gardens nearby, this is the only place in the city where you can see the plains of the Llobregat stretching below. ◈ Map A3 • DA

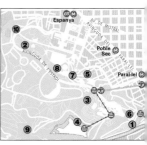

Unless otherwise stated, parks & gardens are usually open 10am-dusk daily.

The Tatami Room

⑩ Restaurants, Cafés, Bars & Clubs

1 Oleum
Dine on refined Mediterranean cuisine under the dome of the Palau Nacional and enjoy the views across the city. ✆ *Palau Nacional • Map B4 • 93 289 06 79 • Closed Sun eve & Mon • DA • €€€€*

2 Bar Seco
A simple café serving cakes and snacks, with more substantial dishes at lunchtime. There's a summer terrace and free Wi-Fi. ✆ *Passeig Montjuïc 74 • Map C5 • 93 329 63 74 • Closed Mon–Wed eve • €€*

3 El Sortidor
With original stained-glass doors and tiled floors from 1908, El Sortidor serves elegant meals fitting in with the romantic setting. ✆ *Plaça del Sortidor 5 • Map C4 • 93 518 95 44 • Closed Mon eve & Tue • €€€*

4 The Tatami Room
Modelled on a Japanese inn, this eatery has all kinds of tasty Japanese dishes, plus curries and noodles. ✆ *C/Poeta Cabanyes 19 • Map C4 • 93 329 67 40 • Closed Mon • €€*

5 La Tomaquera
A neighbourhood classic that serves Catalan home cooking at bargain prices. Arrive early or be prepared to queue. ✆ *C/Margarit 58 • Map C4 • Closed dinner Sun, Mon, Aug, Easter week • €€*

6 El Lliure
The Lliure theatre has a good-value café with an adjoining restaurant and terrace. ✆ *Passeig Santa Madrona 40-46 • Map B4 • Open Mon–Fri for lunch and for dinner on days with performances • DA • €€€*

7 La Terrrazza
Dance music rules at one of Barcelona's most popular nightclubs, housed in a Balearic-style mansion. ✆ *Poble Espanyol • Map A3 • Closed Sun, mid-Oct–mid-Jun • Adm • DA*

8 Jon Mai
This bar may not look much, but the tapas and Catalan dishes are tasty, and the set lunch menu is one of the best deals in town. ✆ *Plaça del Sortidor 15 • Map C4 • 650 786 721 • Closed Mon • €€*

9 Restaurant Forestier
This elegant restaurant in the AC Miramar has amazing views. ✆ *Pl. Carlos Ibáñez 3 • Map C5 • 93 281 16 00 • Closed Sun & Mon eves • €€€€€*

10 Quimet & Quimet
This tiny bodega has standing room only, but serves tasty tapas and wonderful wines. ✆ *C/Poeta Cabanyes 25 • Map C4 • 93 442 31 42 • Closed Sat eve, Sun, Aug • €€€*

Unless otherwise stated, all restaurants accept credit cards. Admission to Poble Espanyol is free if you have a restaurant reservation.

Left **L'Aquàrium** Right **Swing Bridge, between La Rambla & Moll D'Espanya**

Port Vell, Barceloneta & Port Olímpic

THE HEADY ALLURE OF THE MEDITERRANEAN *permeates Barcelona, and a dip into its azure waters is only a few metro stops (or a brisk walk) away. Barcelona's beaches were once hidden behind an industrial wasteland, but things changed radically in preparation for the 1992 Olympics. The rallying cry was to create a new Barcelona oberta al mar (open to the sea); the result is phenomenal, as is the presence of large crowds seeking sun and sea. Tons of sand were transported to create miles of silky beaches from the fisherman's quarter of Barceloneta to Port Olímpic and beyond. Palm trees were planted, water cleanliness standards implemented and, this being design-obsessed Barcelona, numerous contemporary sculptures erected. The city's first two skyscrapers, the Torre Mapfre office building and the five-star Hotel Arts (see p143), punctuate the port's skyline, while the nearby Port Olímpic throbs with scores of bars, clubs and restaurants.*

Barceloneta beach

Sights & Attractions

1	Beaches	6	Boat & Cable Car Trips
2	Museu d'Història de Catalunya	7	Pailebot Santa Eulàlia
3	Rambla de Mar	8	Submarine Ictíneo II
4	L'Aquàrium	9	El Centre de la Vila-Port Olímpic
5	Barceloneta	10	World Trade Center

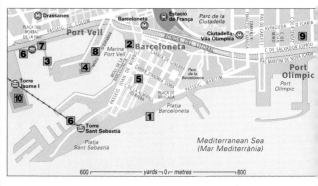

Take a boat tour of the port area See p133

1 Beaches

Fancy a splash in the Mediterranean? Trot down to the end of La Rambla, wander along the palm tree-lined Moll de la Fusta, down restaurant-packed Passeig Joan de Borbó, et voilà, the sea beckons. More than 4 km (2.5 miles) of blue-flag beaches stretch north from Barceloneta to Port Olímpic and beyond. Facilities are top-notch, including showers, deck chairs, beach volleyball courts and lifeguards. Convenience, however, means crowds, so finding a spot among the masses of oiled bodies can be a challenge, particularly in the summer. ◈ *Map E6*

2 Museu d'Història de Catalunya

Housed in the Palau de Mar, a renovated portside warehouse, this museum offers a broad, interactive exploration of Catalonia's history since prehistoric times. Kids *(see p63)* especially will have a ball with the engaging exhibits, such as a Civil War-era bunker and a recreated Catalan bar from the 1960s with an ancient *futbolín* (table football) game. ◈ *Pl Pau Vila 3, Palau de Mar • Map N6 • Open 10am–7pm Tue–Sat (to 8pm Wed), 10am–2:30pm Sun • Adm, free first Sun of month • DA*

3 Rambla de Mar

Saunter along the Rambla de Mar, a floating wooden pier that leads to Maremagnum, a flashy mall that has many shops and restaurants. Nearby the giant IMAX® cinema shows 3-D films on megascreens generally on

Museu d'Història de Catalunya

nature-, adventure- and sports-related topics. ◈ *Moll d'Espanya • Map E5 ◈ Maremagnum: shops open 10am–10pm daily; restaurants until 1am daily ◈ IMAX: shows 10:20am–9pm daily (times vary) • Adm • DA*

4 L'Aquàrium

Come face to face with the marine world of the Mediterranean at the largest aquarium in Europe. The highlight is the 80-m (262-ft) long underwater tunnel, which has a moving walkway that transports visitors through the deep blue unknown, while sharks glide menacingly close. A huge hit with the kids is the Explora! floor, with interactive exhibits that allow you to explore the ecosystems of the Mediterranean. ◈ *Moll d'Espanya • Map E6 • Open Jul & Aug: 9:30am–11pm daily; Sep–Jun: 9:30am–9pm Mon–Fri (to 9:30pm Sat & Sun, Jun & Sep) • Adm • DA*

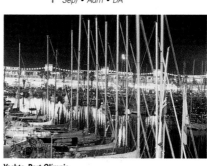

Yachts, Port Olímpic

5 Barceloneta

A portside warren of narrow streets, small squares and ancient bars, this traditional neighbourhood of *pescadors* (fishermen) and *mariners* (sailors) seems worlds apart from the megamalls and disco lights of nearby Port Olímpic. A refreshing foray through this tight-knit community

Yachts & skyscrapers, Port Olímpic

yields a glimpse into the way Barcelona was 150 years ago. Older couples still pull chairs out onto the street to gossip and watch the world go by, and small seafood restaurants serve a *menú del dia* of whatever's fresh off the boat. Running the length of Barceloneta's western edge is Passeig Joan de Borbó, which is lined with restaurants serving *mariscs* (shellfish) and paellas. ◈ *Map F5*

6 Boat & Cable Car Trips

See Barcelona's port activity from a different perspective, either from the air or the sea. The *Transbordador Aeri* cable

Street scene, Barceloneta

cars offer sweeping bird's-eye views of Barcelona and its coast, while the old-fashioned Las Golondrinas boats and the Orsom Catamaran and port area. ◈ *Telefèric, from Torre San Sebastià • Map E6 • Adm ◈ Las Golondrinas, Portal de la Pau • Map E5 • roughly 30 mins from 11:30am • 93 442 31 06 • Adm ◈ Orsom, Portal de la Pau • www.barcelona-orsom. • www.barcelona-orsom.com • Map E5 • Call 93 441 05 37 for times • Adm • DA*

7 Pailebot Santa Eulàlia

Bobbing in the water at the Moll de la Fusta (Timber Quay) is this restored three-mast schooner, originally christened *Carmen Flores*. It first set sail from Spain in 1918. On journeys to Cuba, the ship used to transport textiles and salt, and return with tobacco, coffee, cereals and wood. In 1997, the Museu Marítim *(see p81)* bought and restored the ship as part of an ongoing project to create a collection of seaworthy historical Catalan vessels. ◈ *Moll de la Fusta • Map L6 • Open Apr–Oct: 10am–8:30pm daily (from 2pm Sat); Nov–Mar: 10am–5:30pm Tue–Sun • Adm*

8 Submarine Ictíneo II

In 1859, Catalan Narcís Monturiol invented one of the world's first submarines, a replica of which stands on the Moll d'Espanya. Hard to believe, but in an earlier version of this wooden fish-shaped submarine, powered by two internal steam engines, Monturiol made a number of successful underwater journeys.

He invented the submarine as a means of gathering coral; later, he tried to sell it to the army. However, he finally sold his invention in parts and died penniless. ⊗ *Moll d'Espanya • Map E5*

9 El Centre de la Vila-Port Olímpic

This shopping complex offers a slew of shops, cafés and fast food restaurants. Best of all, it houses the cinemas of the Icària Yelmo Cineplex *(see p67)*, one of the largest cinemas in town to show VO (non-dubbed) films. ⊗ *Salvador Espriu 61 • Map H5* • *Mall shops open 10am–10pm Mon–Sat*

Pailebot Santa Eulàlia

10 World Trade Center

This massive, circular structure is an iconic building in Port Vell. It is home to shops, offices, congress and convention halls and a five-star hotel. In the central courtyard is a "rhythmic" fountain that spurts out streams of water at differing velocities. Nearby, you can board cable cars and soak up splendid views from the top of Torre Jaume I. The terrace has an elegant restaurant, WTC Meet&Eat, which is open for lunch only. ⊗ *Moll de Barcelona • Map D6 • DA*

Exploring the Port

Morning

🕐 Begin your port *passeig* (stroll) with a visit to the **Museu Marítim** *(see p81)*, where you can see Barcelona's status as one of the most active ports in the Mediterranean. From here, head towards the Monument a Colom *(see p12)*, and stroll the Moll de la Fusta to admire the **Pailebot Santa Eulàlia**, which has been immaculately restored by the museum. Saunter down the **Rambla de Mar** *(see p97)*, an undulating wooden drawbridge that leads to the glitzy Maremagnum mega-mall. At the start of the pier, embark on the **Orsom Catamaran**, where you can grab a drink and snack and soak up the rays and the port skyline, while sprawled out on a net just inches above the water. Back on land, about 90 minutes later, stroll down the Moll d'Espanya and turn towards the traditional fisherman's quarter of **Barceloneta**, an atmospheric pocket of narrow streets and timeworn bars. Get a real taste of old-style Barcelona at the boisterous tapas bar, **El Vaso de Oro** (C/Balboa 6). Wedge yourself in at the bar and savour some tasty seafood morsels.

Afternoon

Revived, head to Pg Joan de Borbó and make for the beach. Douse yourself in the Med, then siesta in the afternoon sun. Pick yourself up with sangria at the beachside **Salamanca Chiringuito** (at the end of Pg Joan de Borbó), where you can bury your feet in the sand and watch the waves lap on the shore as the sun dips into the horizon.

You can't miss Frank Gehry's massive, glistening Peix sculpture on Passeig Marítim **See p41**

Left **Club Catwalk** Right **Razzmatazz**

TOP 10 Bars & Beach Clubs

1 Club Catwalk
One of the hottest clubs in town, this has two floors: one for the bar and chilling out, and the other for dancing to hip hop, R 'n' B, electronica and house. ◊ *Ramón Trías Fargas 2–4 • Map G6 • Closed Mon • DA • Adm*

2 CDLC
Right by the beach, with a terrace on which to relax, this is a restaurant that becomes a club after dinner. Guest DJs feature every week. ◊ *Passeig Marítim de la Barceloneta 32 • Map G6*

3 Bar Jai Ca
The TV blares and kids race around in this relaxed neighbourhood favourite. Delicious tapas are on offer. ◊ *C/Ginebra 13 • Map F5 • 93 268 32 65 • Closed Mon*

4 Boo
This restaurant, cocktail lounge and beach club offers drinks, tapas, live music and DJ sessions. ◊ *Espigó de Bac de Roda 1, Platja Nova Mar Bella • 93 225 01 00 • DA*

5 Arola
A luxurious, summer-only poolside bar at the plush Hotel Arts, the Arola has huge white beds covered with silk cushions, DJ sessions, and a range of perfectly mixed cocktails. ◊ *C/Marina 19–21 • Map G5 • 93 483 80 90*

6 Le Kasbah
With Arabic decoration, soft lights and house music, this bar

in the Palau del Mar building provides a city oasis. ◊ *Plaça de Pau Vila 1 • Map F6 • Closed Mon*

7 Mar Bella beach bars
Head to one of the *xiringuitos* (beach bars) on Barcelona's hippest beach and enjoy the DJ sessions. ◊ *Platja Nova Mar Bella • Open only in summer*

8 Eclipse
The spectacular bar on the 26th floor of the landmark Hotel Vela offers magnificent views of the city. Cocktail attire dress code. ◊ *Hotel Vela Plaça de la Rosa dels Vents 1 • Map F6 • 93 295 28 00*

9 Shôko
Doubling as a Japanese restaurant during the day, this club by the beach provides all kinds of music in a great setting. ◊ *Passeig Marítim de la Barceloneta 36 • Map E6*

10 Razzmatazz
Concerts – from rock to jazz – feature several nights a week at this trendy club, which boasts five spaces offering a range of musical styles, such as the Razz Club and the Loft. ◊ *C/Almogàvers 122 (The Loft: C/Pamplona 88) • Map H4 • Razz Club and Loft closed Sun–Tue*

For Barcelona's best nightlife See pp46–7

Price Categories

For a three-course meal for one with half a bottle of wine (or equivalent meal), taxes and extra charges.

€	under €15
€€	€15–25
€€€	€25–35
€€€€	€35–45
€€€€€	over €45

Agua

🔟 Restaurants & Tapas Bars

1 Set Portes
Founded in 1836, this large institution serves some of the finest Catalan cuisine in the city, including paellas. ✆ *Pg Isabel II 14* • *Map N5* • *93 319 30 33* • *DA* • *€€€€€*

2 Agua
The spacious terrace at this restaurant boasts views of the sea. Superb seafood and Mediterranean fare feature on the menu. ✆ *Pg Marítim 30* • *Map G6* • *93 225 12 72* • *DA* • *€€€€*

3 Can Manel la Puda
The oldest restaurant on this strip serves Catalan cuisine, specializing in catch-of-the-day dishes. ✆ *Pg Joan de Borbó 60–61* • *Map F6* • *93 221 50 13* • *Closed Mon* • *DA* • *€€€*

4 Somorrostro
This chic restaurant serves a daily changing menu prepared with fresh ingredients. Warm ambience and decor. ✆ *Sant Carles 11* • *Map F6* • *93 225 00 10* • *Closed lunch (except Sun), Tue, 2 weeks Jan* • *€€€*

5 Kaiku
Decorated with fishing nets, Kaiku is renowned for its seafood, especially the *arros del xef* (chef's rice). ✆ *Plaça del Mar 1* • *Map E6* • *93 221 90 82* • *Closed eve, Mon* • *€€€*

6 Salamanca
This may feel like a tourist trap at first, but the food is top notch. There are plenty of meat dishes on offer. ✆ *C/Almirall Cervera 34* • *Map F6* • *93 221 50 33* • *€€€€*

7 Can Ganassa
An old-style, family-run tapas bar that has been serving fresh seafood tapas to locals for decades. ✆ *Pl de la Barceloneta 4–6* • *Map F6* • *93 221 75 86* • *€*

8 La Mar Salada
This light, bright restaurant near the sea serves modern fare with the emphasis on seafood, including monkfish with wild mushrooms and artichokes, and paella. The weekday set lunch menu (€15.50) is great value. ✆ *Passeig de Joan de Borbó 58* • *Map E6* • *93 221 21 27* • *Closed Tue* • *€€€€*

9 Suquet de l'Almirall
This family-run gem serves excellent *arroz de barca* (rice in broth, with seafood) and *suquet* (seafood and potato stew). ✆ *Pg Joan de Borbó 65* • *Map F6* • *93 221 62 33* • *Closed Sun eve, Mon, lunch in Aug* • *DA* • *€€€€€*

10 La Bombeta
This traditional bar offers a wonderful glimpse of life in Barcelona before the tourists arrived. The house speciality is the *bombas*, deep-fried balls of mashed potatoes served with a spicy tomato sauce. ✆ *C/Maquinista 33* • *Map F6* • *93 319 94 95* • *€*

Unless otherwise stated, all restaurants accept credit cards. For tips on dining and standard opening hours See p138

101

Left **Fountain, Rambla de Catalunya** Right *Modernista* hotel entrance

Eixample

I F THE OLD TOWN IS THE HEART of Barcelona and the green mountains of Tibidabo and Montjuïc the lungs, the Eixample is the city's nervous system – its economic and commercial core. The area began to take shape in 1860 when the city was permitted to expand beyond the medieval walls (see p30). Its design, based on plans by Catalan engineer Ildefons Cerdà, comprises hundreds of symmetrical grid-like squares. Construction continued into the 20th century at a time when Barcelona's elite was patronizing the city's most daring architects. Modernisme was flourishing and the area became home to the cream of Barcelona's Modernista architecture, with myriad elegant façades and balconies. Today, a wealth of enchanting cafés, funky design shops, gourmet restaurants and hip bars and clubs draws the professional crowd, which has adopted the neighbourhood as its own.

🔟 Sights

1. Sagrada Família
2. La Pedrera
3. Mansana de la Discòrdia
4. Hospital de la Santa Creu i de Sant Pau
5. Fundació Tàpies
6. Palau Baró de Quadras
7. Fundació Francisco Godia
8. Rambla de Catalunya
9. Disseny Hub
10. Museu Egipci

Spires, Sagrada Família

For more on Modernista *architecture* **See pp32–3**

Sagrada Família
Gaudí's wizardry culminated in this enchanting, wild, unconventional temple, which dominates the city skyline *(see pp8–10)*.

La Pedrera
A daring, surreal fantasyland, and Gaudí's most remarkable civic work *(see pp20–21)*.

Windows, Casa Batlló, Mansana de la Discòrdia

Mansana de la Discòrdia
At the heart of the city's *Quadrat d'Or* (Golden Square) lies this stunning block of houses. Literally "the block of discord", the Mansana de la Discòrdia is so-called because of the dramatic contrast of its three flagship buildings. Built between 1900 and 1907 by the three *Modernista* greats, rival architects Gaudí, Domènech i Montaner and Puig i Cadafalch, the buildings were commissioned by competing bourgeois families. Domènech is represented by the ornate Casa Lleó Morera *(see p33)*; Puig makes his mark with the Gothic-inspired Casa Amatller *(see p33)*; and Gaudí flaunts his architectural prowess with Casa Batlló *(see p33)*. All boast superb interiors, but Casa Lleó Morera is closed to the public. Casa Amatller runs tours of the top floor studio and the exhibition area. The houses at Nos. 37 and 39 add to the overall splendour of the block. The Perfume Museum is at No. 39 *(see p41)*. ✆ Pg de Gràcia 35–45 • Map E2

Hospital de la Santa Creu i de Sant Pau
A fully functioning hospital until 2010, it was built in two stages from 1905 by Domènech i Montaner and his son. A tribute to *Modernisme* – and Domènech's answer to Gaudí's Sagrada Família – the design includes eight pavilions and various other buildings linked by underground tunnels. The pavilions recall the history of Catalonia with murals, mosaics and sculptures. Interlacing the buildings are beautiful gardens, which are open to visitors, along with the courtyards. Part of the Ruta del Modernisme *(see p133)*. ✆ C/Sant Antoni Maria Claret 167 • Map H1 • 93 317 76 52 • Guided visits in English 10am, 11am, noon & 1pm daily • Adm

Left **Hospital de la Santa Creu i de Sant Pau** Right **Casa Lleó Morera, Mansana de la Discòrdia**

Main entrance, Fundació Francisco Godia

5 Fundació Tàpies

Paintings and sculptures by Antoni Tàpies (b. 1923), Catalonia's foremost living artist, are housed in this early *Modernista* building *(see p32)*. For a glimpse of what awaits inside, look up: crowning the museum is the artist's eye-catching wire sculpture *Cloud & Chair* (1990). The collection of over 300 pieces covers Tàpies' whole range of work, including impressive abstract pieces such as *Grey Ochre on Brown* (1962). Temporary exhibitions are also held here, with past shows by Mario Herz, Hans Hacke and Craigie Horsfield. ֎ *C/Aragó 255 • Map E2 • 93 487 03 15 • Open 10am–7pm Tue–Sun • Adm • DA • Free under 16*

6 Palau Baró de Quadras

Built by the architect Puig i Cadafalch, this *Modernista* mansion has a Gothic influence with its medieval-style turrets adorned with gargoyles. The mansion now houses the Casa Asia, and is open to the public for regular exhibitions on Asian themes. The building is located between two important streets and has two completely different façades. ֎ *Avda Diagonal 373 • Map E2 • 93 368 08 36 • Open 10am–8pm Tue–Sat*

Ildefons Cerdà

Ildefons Cerdà's design for the new city, comprising a uniform grid of square blocks, received backing in 1859. Reflecting Cerdà's utopian socialist ideals, each block was to have a garden-like courtyard, surrounded by uniform flats. Real estate vultures soon intervened and the court-yards were converted into warehouses and factories. Today these green spaces are gradually being reinstated.

7 Fundació Francisco Godia

Although Francisco Godia (1921–90) was best known as an F1 racing driver, his passions extended to the art world. His private collection now forms this museum, housed in a beautiful *Modernista* mansion designed by Enric Sagnier, and encompasses a range of art from medieval times to the 20th century: from Jaume Huguet's altarpiece *St Mary Magdalene* (c. 1445) to a range of Spanish ceramics and works by 17th-century fresco-painter Luca Giordano. ֎ *C/Diputació 250 • Map E3 • 93 272 31 80 • Open 10am–8pm Wed–Mon • Adm*

Cloud & Chair sculpture, Fundació Tàpies

Rambla de Catalunya

This elegant extension of the better-known Rambla is a more up-market version. Lined with trees that form a leafy green tunnel in summer, it boasts scores of pretty façades and shops, including the *Modernista* Farmàcia Bolos (No. 77). The avenue teems with terrace bars and cafés, which are ideal for people-watching. *See also p50.* ⊗ *Map E2*

Museu Egipci

Disseny Hub

Due to open in spring 2014, the Disseny Hub Barcelona (DHUB) will be a design museum and gallery, showcasing fashion design, architecture, graphic design communication and product design. It will also host regular themed talks helping to promote the design world.
⊗ *Pl de la Glòries 137 • Map H3 • 93 309 15 40 • Call in advance for opening times*

Museu Egipci

Spain's most important Egyptology museum houses more than 350 exhibits from over 3,000 years of Ancient Egypt. Exhibits include terracotta figures, human and animal mummies, and a bust of the lion goddess Sekhmet (700–300 BC). ⊗ *C/València 284 • Map E2 • Open 10am–8pm Mon–Sat, 10am–2pm Sun • 93 488 01 88 • www. museuegipci.com • Adm*

The Modernista Route

Morning

Visit the **Museu del Modernisme Català** (C/Balmes 48, Tel: 93 272 28 96) for an introduction to Catalan Art Nouveau through a series of fascinating temporary exhibitions, then stroll around the gardens of the Universitat. Head east along Gran Via past the elegant Palace Barcelona Hotel *(see p143)* and right down C/Bruc for a glimpse of Gaudí's **Casa Calvet** *(see p109)* on C/Casp. Turn right onto C/Casp and walk three blocks west to the majestic Pg de Gràcia; then go right again three blocks to the impressive buildings known as the **Mansana de la Discòrdia** *(see p103)* and the **Perfume Museum** *(see p41)*. Sniff around **Regia** perfume shop *(see p106)* before continuing north to marvel at Gaudí's **La Pedrera** *(see pp20–21)*. Feeling peckish? Stop at **Windsor** on C/Còrsega (cnr Rambla de Catalunya) *(see p109)*. The set menu is an enjoyable way to experience Catalan *haute cuisine*.

Afternoon

After lunch, head north on Pg de Gràcia, turn right along Diagonal, taking in the fairy-tale **Casa de les Punxes** at No. 416 *(see p33)*. Walk along Diagonal, making a detour left at Pg Sant Joan to see **Palau Macaya** at No. 108. Then stroll along C/Mallorca to the **Sagrada Família** *(see pp8–11)*. Here you can take in the Nativity Façade and rest weary legs in the Plaça de Gaudí before climbing the bell towers for a breathtaking view of the city.

Around Town – Eixample

Left **Light, Dos i Una** Centre **Shoppers, Passeig de Gràcia** Right **Furniture, Vinçon**

Design Shops

1 Vinçon
The cream of the crop in Spanish design with out-of-this-world designs for the most everyday objects. Furniture is displayed in a 1900 upper-class apartment. Breathtaking.
◈ Pg de Gràcia 96 • Map E2

2 L'Appartement
A spacious, white-painted store packed with gorgeous furnishings and knick-knacks at reasonable prices: from quirky, cool lights and sculptures to bags, jewellery and t-shirts. ◈ C/Enric Granados 44 • Map E2 • Closed Sun

3 Regia
The biggest perfume shop in the city has over one thousand scents, including all the leading brands and other surprises. Also home to the Perfume Museum (see p41). ◈ Pg de Gràcia 39 • Map E2

4 Dos i Una
A designer gift shop with a steel-tiled floor and a psychedelic colour scheme. Concentrates on selling "made in Barcelona" items, which make for unusual souvenirs.
◈ C/Rosselló 275 • Map E2

5 Muxart
Excellent and arty shoe shop for men, women and kids in a country famed for its leather.
◈ C/Rosselló 230 • Map E2

6 Biosca & Botey
Exceptionally elegant shop selling all kinds of lamps, from Art-Nouveau mushrooms to ultramodern steel shades.
◈ Av Diagonal 458 • Map E2 • DA

7 Pilma
Breathtaking designer shop selling quality modern furniture and interior accessories by big names, as well as cutting-edge creations by Catalan designers.
◈ Av Diagonal 403 • Map E1

8 DBarcelona
An eclectic range of gadgets and gifts in a shop that doubles as an exhibition space for up-and-coming designers and more established artists.
◈ Av Diagonal 367 • Map F2

9 Kowasa
A specialist photography bookshop with over 7,000 titles, including foreign magazines. The ambience is friendly and intimate and browsing is encouraged.
◈ C/Mallorca 235 • Map E2 • DA

10 Bagués Joieria
Every piece on sale at this iconic, renowned jewellery shop (established 1839) is handmade using traditional methods. ◈ Passeig de Gràcia 41 • Map E2 • Closed Sun

Left **Dance Floor, City Hall** Right **OmmSessions Club**

After-Dark Venues

Milano
1 Red velvet sofas and expertly mixed cocktails make this an excellent option for late night drinks. There are occasional live jazz performances. ✪ *Ronda Universitat 35 • Map E3 • Open noon–2:30am daily*

Xixbar
2 A small bar with a big reputation. The gin and tonics, prepared with a vast range of gins sold in the shop next door, are considered the best in the city. ✪ *C/Rocafort 19 • Map C4*

Dry Martini
3 A classic and elegant venue where extraordinarily professional barmen are ready to prepare your favourite cocktail. Quiet jazz sounds play in the background. ✪ *C/Aribau 162 • Map D2*

OmmSessions Club
4 In one of the most fashionable addresses in town, this club attracts a young, international crowd. ✪ *C/Rosselló 265 • Map E2 • Closed Sun, Mon, Tue & 3 wks in Aug*

Bar Marfil
5 Part of the Hotel Murmuri, this is a fashionable bar on a fancy shopping street. Sink into a plush faux-Baroque armchair and sip a delectable cocktail. ✪ *Rambla de Catalunya 104 • Map E2*

Luz de Gas
6 A classic late-night watering hole, this half concert hall, half bar has live music nightly – from blues to jazz and soul. ✪ *C/Muntaner 246 • Map D1 • DA*

Ideal
7 Luxurious cocktail lounge opened by legendary barman José María Gotarda in 1931 and now run by his son. More than 80 varieties of whisky. ✪ *C/Aribau 89 • Map D2 • Closed Sun*

City Hall
8 This popular club has two dance floors. Club nights cover a range of music styles, from electro pop to drum 'n' bass. ✪ *Rambla de Catalunya 2-4 • Map E3 • Closed Mon*

Museum
9 This is one of the hottest gay bars in town. The black-and-gold faux Baroque decor is offset with huge video screens. ✪ *C/Sepúlveda 178 • Map D3 (Sepúlveda) • Open 10pm–3am daily • Closed 3 wks in Feb*

Les Gens que j'Aime
10 The ideal place to have a drink while enjoying soft music, after walking around Passeig de Gràcia and Rambla Catalunya. ✪ *Valencia 286 • Map E2 • Open 6pm–2:30am daily (3am weekends)*

Left **Laie Llibrería Cafè** Right **Casa Alfonso**

🔟 Cafés

1 Laie Llibrería Cafè
A cultural meeting place with a lively atmosphere, airy terrace and one of the best bookshops in town. There's an excellent set lunch. ◈ *C/Pau Claris 85 • Map E3 • Closed Sun*

2 Cafè del Centre
Said to be the oldest café in the Eixample, with dark wooden interiors that have not changed for a century. An unpretentious spot for a quiet coffee. ◈ *C/Girona 69 • Map F3 • Closed Sun*

3 Casa Alfonso
This classy café has been in business since 1929. Arguably the best *pernil* (serrano ham) in the city. ◈ *C/Roger de Llúria 6 • Map F3 • Closed Sun*

4 Cacao Sampaka
An infinite array of chocolate, including innovative combinations such as chocolate with Parmesan cheese or olive oil. ◈ *C/Consell de Cent 292 • Map E3 • Closed Sun, mornings in Aug*

5 Mauri
One of the best pastry shops in town. Enjoy a hot drink with an elaborate dessert in *Modernista* surroundings. ◈ *Rambla Catalunya 102 • Map E2 • Closed Sun from 3pm*

6 Galeria Cosmo
Located on a semi-pedestri-anized street, this art gallery café offers sandwiches, cakes and tapas. Free Wi-Fi. ◈ *C/Enric*

Granados 3 • Map E2 • Open 9am–11pm Mon–Thu, 10am–midnight Fri, noon–midnight Sat, noon–10pm Sun

7 Cornelia & Co.
Come to this great spot near the Passeig de Gràcia for brunch, coffee and cakes, or a light meal, and pick up some deli goodies. ◈ *C/Valencia 225 • Map E2*

8 Velódromo
This historic bar with original 1930s furnishings was reopened by local celebrity chef Charles Abellan. The menu features sophisticated versions of Catalan classics. ◈ *C/Muntaner 213 • Map D1 • 93 430 60 22*

9 Mantequería Ravell
A deli-style shop offering incredible breakfasts, including eggs with *foie gras*, at a huge communal table. Wine and traditional hams and cheeses are also available. ◈ *C/Aragó 313 • Map F2*

10 Joséphine
Coffee and snacks are served all day at this French colonial café. There's also an evening menu. ◈ *C/Pau Claris 147 • Map E2 • Closed Sun*

Price Categories

For a three-course meal for one with half a bottle of wine (or equivalent meal), taxes and extra charges.

€	under €15
€€	€15–25
€€€	€25–35
€€€€	€35–45
€€€€€	over €45

Casa Calvet

🔟 Restaurants & Tapas Bars

1 Windsor
Modern Catalan *haute cuisine* is served in elegant surroundings with chandeliers and red upholstered furniture. There's also a garden for alfresco dining. ✆ C/Còrsega 286 • Map E1 • 93 237 75 88 • Closed Sun, 1st week in Jan, Easter Week, Aug • DA • €€€€€

2 Monvinic
An ultra-modern wine bar serving a global choice of wines. They also have excellent tapas and more substantial fare. ✆ C/Diputació 249 • Map E3 • 93 272 61 87 • Closed Sat & Sun, Aug • €€€

3 Cinc Sentits
Indulge the five senses (*cinc sentits* in Catalan) at this stylish restaurant offering modern interpretations of classic Catalan cuisine. ✆ C/Aribau 58 • Map D2 • 93 323 94 90 • Closed Sun & Mon • €€€€€

4 Moments
The menu at this sleek restaurant in the ultra-luxurious Mandarin Oriental hotel includes sublime contemporary renditions of Catalan classics, from tartare of langoustine to scallops with artichokes. ✆ Passeig de Gràcia 38–40 • Map E3 • 93 151 87 81 • Closed Sun & Mon • €€€€€

5 Igueldo
Modern Basque cuisine is served in elegant surroundings, and there's a tapas counter too. ✆ Rosselló 186 • Map E2 • 93 452 25 55 • Closed Sun • DA • €€€€€

6 Casa Calvet
Catalan food with a modern twist is served in Gaudí-designed dining rooms. ✆ C/Casp 48 • Map F3 • 93 412 40 12 • Closed Sun & pub hols • DA • €€€€€

7 Moo
Run by the Roca brothers, Moo serves creative Catalan fare. Book in advance. ✆ C/Rosselló 265 • Map E2 • 93 445 40 00 • Closed Sun, 2 weeks Jan, 2 weeks Aug • DA • €€€€€

8 La Taverna del Clínic
The menu at this unassuming bar includes both old classics and excellent contemporary tapas. ✆ C/Rosselló 155 • Map D2 • 93 410 42 21 • Closed Sat lunch & Sun • €€€

9 Cervecería Catalana
Just a few steps from Rambla de Catalunya, with some of the best tapas in town and a variety of beers. ✆ C/Mallorca 236 • Map E2 • 93 216 03 68 • DA • €€€

10 Paco Meralgo
This bright, modern tapas bar has a gourmet menu based on recipes from around the country. ✆ C/Muntaner 171 • Map D1 • 93 430 90 27 • DA • €€

Unless otherwise stated, all restaurants accept credit cards. For tips on dining and standard opening hours See p138

109

Left **Cloister, Monestir de Pedralbes** Right **CosmoCaixa Museu de la Ciència**

Gràcia, Tibidabo & Zona Alta

THE ZONA ALTA *(Uptown)* is an area covering several neighbourhoods that, as the name suggests, are in the hilly part of the city. From the moneyed streets of Pedralbes and Tibidabo to bohemian Gràcia, this entire northern area of the city offers stunning views and regal attractions. But what really sets this area apart from the rest of the city is its 15 parks; the best are Gaudí's stunning and imaginative Parc Güell, and the colossal natural park of Collserola, which spreads out like green baize over Tibidabo mountain. Gràcia stands out as the city's most cosmopolitan neighbourhood. Its strong political tradition and gypsy community have long drawn artists and writers to the labyrinthine streets, and it is now home to scores of innovative boutiques, bars and squares, which teem with life most nights of the week.

Parc d'Atraccions del Tibidabo

🔟 Sights & Attractions

1. Parc d'Atraccions del Tibidabo
2. Monestir de Pedralbes
3. Torre de Collserola
4. Camp Nou Experience
5. CosmoCaixa Museu de la Ciència
6. Parc Güell
7. Temple Expiatori del Sagrat Cor
8. Parc de Collserola
9. Tramvia Blau
10. Jardins del Laberint d'Horta

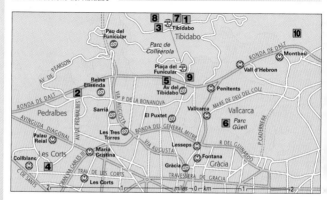

The best way to visit this area is on the Bus Turístic **See p133**

1 Parc d'Atraccions del Tibidabo

Take the funicular up to the top of Tibidabo's 517-m (1,695-ft) mountain to visit this traditional amusement park, which opened in 1908. There are a couple of stomach-churning, white-knuckle rides, but the real attractions are the quaint, old-fashioned ones, including a beautifully conserved carousel and a Ferris wheel. Here also is the Museu dels Autòmates *(see p41)*, with automatons, mechanical models and a scale model of the park. ◈ *Pl de Tibidabo • Map B1 • Opening times vary, see the website for details • www.tibidabo.cat • Adm • DA*

2 Monestir de Pedralbes

Named after the Latin *petras albas*, which means white stones, this outstandingly beautiful Gothic monastery was founded by Queen Elisenda de Montcada de Piños in the early 14th century. Her alabaster tomb lies in the wall between the church and the impressive three-storey Gothic cloister. An interesting glimpse of medieval life is provided by the furnished kitchens, cells, infirmary and refectory, which are all well preserved. ◈ *C/Baixada Monestir 9 • Map A1 • Open from 10am Tue–Sun. Closes: Apr–Sep at 5pm Tue–Fri, 7pm Sat, 8pm Sun; Oct–Mar at 2pm Tue–Fri, 5pm Sat & Sun • Adm; free 1st Sun of the month and every Sun 3–8pm • DA*

3 Torre de Collserola

This slender telecommunications tower was designed by British architect Norman Foster.

Torre de Collserola

The needle-like upper structure rests on a concrete pillar and is anchored by 12 huge steel cables. Rising to a height of 560 m (1836 ft) above sea level, the top is reached by a glass-fronted elevator. On a clear day, you can see Montserrat and the Pyrenees. ◈ *Parc de Collserola • Map B1 • Check website for opening hours. • www.torrede collserola.com • Adm • DA*

4 Camp Nou Experience

The Museu del FC Barcelona, Barcelona's most visited museum, is a must for fans of the beautiful game. With football memorabilia of every kind, you can learn all about the club. Work donated by some of Catalonia's leading artists is also on display. Admission includes access to Barça's 120,000-seater stadium, Camp Nou, an impressive monument to the city's love affair with the game. ◈ *Entrance 9 Stadium, Av Arístides Maillol • Map A2 • Open 10am–6:30pm Mon–Sat (to 7:30pm Apr–Oct), 10am–2:30pm Sun • Adm • DA (times vary)*

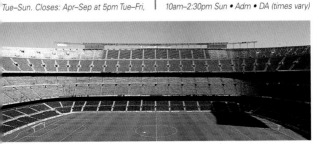

Camp Nou Stadium

Gràcia

Until the late 19th century, Gràcia was a fiercely proud independent city. Despite locals' protests, it became part of Barcelona proper in 1898, but has always maintained a sense of separatism and has been a hotbed of political activity. It is now home to a booming cottage industry nurtured by a growing band of artisans. Don't miss the *barri*'s annual fiesta *(see p65)* in the second week of August.

Spiral entrance ramp at CosmoCaixa

5 CosmoCaixa Museu de la Ciència

Barcelona's science museum is a thoroughly stimulating and inter-active affair. It occupies a glass-and-steel building, with six of its nine storeys set underground. Displays include a wide range of historic objects, flora and fauna. One of its most important pieces is a recreated section of flooded Amazon forest, with fish, reptiles, mammals, birds and plants. A tour through Earth's geological history explains processes such as erosion and sedimentation. There are also innovative temporary exhibitions on environmental issues. See p41.
⊗ *C/Isaac Newton 26 • Map B1 • 93 212 60 50 • Open 10am–8pm Tue–Sun (summer & Christmas: also Mon) • Adm (free 1st Sun of the month) • DA*

6 Parc Güell

A UNESCO World Heritage Site, this heady brew of archi-tectural wizardry includes *trencadís* tiling, fairy-tale pavilions, Gothic archways, and the column-ed Sala Hipóstila (originally meant as a market hall). In true Gaudí style, playfulness and symbolism pervade every aspect of the park. The Casa-Museu Gaudí, where Gaudí lived for 20 years, is dedicated to the architect's life.
⊗ *C/d'Olot • Map B2 • Open 8am–9pm daily • Free* ⊗ *Casa-Museu Gaudí • Map B2 • Open Apr–Sep: 10am–7:45pm; Oct–Mar: 10am–5:45pm • Adm (combined ticket with Sagrada Família available)*

7 Temple Expiatori del Sagrat Cor

Visible from almost anywhere in Barcelona, the Temple of the Sa-cred Heart was built by Enric Sag-nier between 1902 and 1911. It has a dramatic sculpture of Jesus and an elaborately decorated door. Take the elevator up the main tower, or climb the steps to the outside terrace for breathtaking views. ⊗ *Pl del Tibidabo • Map B1 • 93 417 56 86 • Open 10am–8pm daily (Elevator open 10:30am–2pm & 3–7pm daily) • Adm*

View, Temple Expiatori del Sagrat Cor

Parc del Laberint d'Horta

8 Parc de Collserola

Beyond the peaks of Tibidabo mountain, this 6,500-ha (16,000-acre) natural park of wild forest and winding paths is an oasis of calm. It is great for hiking and biking *(see p59)*, with sign-posted paths and nature trails. ✎ *Info point: C/Església 92 • Map B1 • 93 280 35 52 • www.parcnaturalcollserola.cat*

9 Tramvia Blau

The city's blue trams, with their old-fashioned, wooden interiors are attractions in themselves. The route, from the FGC station to Plaça Doctor Andreu, passes many *Modernista* mansions to the top of Avinguda Tibidabo. ✎ *Av Tibidabo • Map B1 • Trams run Easter, Jul & Aug: 10am–6pm daily (Easter: to 8pm); rest of year: 10am–8pm Sat & Sun (Jan–Mar: to 6pm) • Adm*

10 Parc del Laberint d'Horta

In 1802, the Marquès d'Alfarràs hosted a huge party in these wonderful Neo-Classical gardens to celebrate the visit of Carles IV. Designed by Italian architect Domenico Bagotti, they incorporate a lake, a waterfall, canals and a cypress-tree maze. ✎ *C/German Desvalls • Map C1 • Open 10am–dusk daily • Adm (free Wed & Sun)*

Exploring the Heights

Morning

Taking the northern route of the Bus Turístic *(see p133)* is the easiest way to negotiate the vast northern area of the city; it also gives discounts on entrance to major sights en route. Start off at Plaça de Catalunya (tickets can be bought on board) and sit on the top deck for a good view of the *Modernista* magic along Pg de Gràcia. Make the whimsical **Parc Güell** your first stop and spend the morning ambling around Gaudí's other-worldly park. Get back on the bus and continue north to the southern end of Av Tibidabo. Walk about 500 m (1600 ft) up Av Tibidabo and stop off for a leisurely lunch in the garden of the palatial **El Asador d'Aranda** *(see p117)*.

Afternoon

After you've had your fill of fine Castilian cuisine, continue strolling up Av Tibidabo to Plaça Doctor Andreu where you can hop on the steep funicular train to Plaça de Tibidabo. Pop into the **Parc d'Atraccions** *(see p111)* for a ride on the dodgems or the Ferris wheel. Then head to the landmark **Torre de Collserola** *(see p111)*, where a glass elevator whisks you up to an observation deck for spectacular views. Return to Plaça Doctor Andreu on the funicular and treat yourself to a *granissat* *(see p43)* in one of the terrace bars. Then go down Av Tibidabo on the charming **Tramvia Blau** and catch the Bus Turístic back to the city centre.

Left **Món de Mones** Right **El Piano**

TOP 10 Gràcia Boutiques

1 Érase Una Vez
The name means "once upon a time", and indeed many a storybook fantasy comes true at this shop, which creates fabulous, one-of-a-kind wedding gowns. It also stocks some of the most exclusive designers.
◈ C/Goya 7

2 Ninas
Nina, an American designer, sells simple, modern women's clothes made from fine fabrics. The shop is housed in a gorgeous *Modernista* building which was once a butcher's, and has a workshop at the back. ◈ C/Verdi 39

3 Llena eres de Gràcia
For gorgeous women's fashions, accessories and evening wear at surprisingly reasonable prices, try this colourful boutique. The clothes are very wearable but most have a quirky twist.
◈ C/Ros de Olano 50

4 José Rivero
José provides his own original in-house creations for men and women; he also sells crafted accessories, including handbags, by young local designers. ◈ C/Astúries 43

5 Agua Patagona
Here you'll find original handmade leather shoes for men and children. Comfortable, trendy and reasonably priced, they are sold only here and in Buenos Aires. ◈ Gran de Gràcia 107

6 Món de Mones
For colourful jewellery and accessories, try the "World of Monkeys" (*món de mones* in Catalan) near the Plaça del Sol. The designer, Teresa Roig, uses a variety of materials from glass to felt to create her original designs. ◈ C/Xiquets de Valls 9

7 Camiseria Pons
One of the oldest shops in this area, this men's specialist shop sells shirts by top Spanish and international designers, including Ralph Lauren.
◈ Gran de Gràcia 49

8 Mushi Mushi
From hard-to-find, small labels to the best international collections, this pretty little boutique stocks a fine selection of women's fashion. It also offers a small range of shoes, bags and accessories. ◈ Plaça de la Vila de Gràcia 5

9 El Piano
El Piano sells elegant and stylish women's clothes with a retro flair made by Catalan designer Tina García. It also stocks clothes by other independent designers. ◈ C/Verdi 20 bis

10 Zucca
One of two branches in Barcelona, Zucca offers a superb range of colourful fashion accessories. The stock includes plastic flowers for your hair and stick-on navel rings.
◈ C/Torrent de l'Olla 175

Left **Sign, Cafè Salambó** Centre **La Cafetera** Right **Suís**

Gràcia Cafés

1 Cafè del Sol
This café-bar is a cut above the others in the lively, bohemian Plaça del Sol. The atmosphere buzzes, the conversation inspires and the excellent coffee keeps on coming. ◈ *Pl del Sol 16 • DA*

2 Cafè Salambó
Scrumptious sandwiches and a tasty range of salads are the draw at this beautiful, wooden bar-cum-café. There are pool tables upstairs. ◈ *C/Torrijos 51 • DA*

3 Bar Quimet
An authentic, old-fashioned bar with marble-topped tables and big wooden barrels, this is a great spot for an aperitif. Try the *vermut* and a selection of olives and *boquerones* (fresh anchovies). ◈ *C/Vic 23 • Map E1*

4 La Cafetera
Of all the cafés on Plaça de la Virreina, this one, with its outdoor terrace and tiny patio full of potted plants, is perhaps the most pleasant for a quiet and leisurely morning coffee and a sandwich or pastry. ◈ *Pl de la Virreina 2*

5 Suís
A colourful café that sells great ice creams and fresh fruit juices in summer, plus hot chocolate (which, with added whipped cream, is known as a *suís*) and a wide range of teas in winter. There are also cakes and brownies. ◈ *Travessera de Gràcia 151 • DA*

6 Vreneli
The cosy Plaça de la Vila de Gràcia boasts several café terraces. Vreneli is the most interesting, with a mixture of Mexican, Swiss and Spanish fare. No alcohol is served. ◈ *Pl de la Vila de Gràcia 8 • Closed Mon • DA*

7 Blues Cafè
The walls at this dusky, atmospheric café-bar are plastered with black-and-white photos of John Lee Hooker and Leadbelly, among others. The music, electric or acoustic, is always the blues. ◈ *C/Perla 37*

8 Cafè del Teatre
This is an ideal place to find a young, friendly crowd and good conversation. The only connection with the theatre here seems to be the velvet curtains on the sign over the door of this scruffy, but busy café. ◈ *C/Torrijos 41*

9 La Nena
This café is popular with parents, thanks to the room with tables and games for children. Their range of home-made cakes, juices and hot drinks makes this a neighbourhood favourite. ◈ *C/Ramón y Cajal 36 • Map F1*

10 A Casa Portuguesa
This modern café serves traditional Portuguese pastries, including Belem tarts. There's also a great selection of cheeses, wines and preserves. ◈ *Carrer de Verdi 58 • Map F1 • Closed Mon*

Left **Bobby Gin** Right **Gràcia nightlife, Plaça del Sol**

Hip Drinking Spots

Bobby Gin
This cocktail bar stocks some 60 premium gins – floral, citric, spiced and vintage. Their slogan, "Respect the gin", is courtesy of the famed eponymous bartender. ✆ C/Francisco Giner 47 • Map E1 • DA

Universal Café
Open until 5:30am, Universal Café is a late-night, two-level bar with a spacious, airy interior. The image-concious crowd comes to flirt and dance to house (upstairs) and acid jazz (below). ✆ C/Marià Cubí 182 • Closed Sun • Occasional adm

Mirablau
A slightly older, well-heeled set, who adhere to the smart dress code, come to this club-bar for a combination of cocktails and amazing views of the city. ✆ Pl Dr Andreu • Open from 11am daily

Elephant
Lavish, stylish and totally unique, Elephant is one of the best clubs in the city for a fun night out. In summer, you can lounge in the garden on huge, white beds. ✆ Passeig dels Til.lers 1 • Open from 11:30pm Thu–Sat

Bar Elèctric
A longstanding favourite on the Gràcia scene, Bar Elèctric is a bar as well as a small venue for rock, pop and world music gigs. This cheerful, scruffy neighbourhood bar is packed at weekends. ✆ Travessera de Gràcia 233 • Map D1 • Open from 7pm daily

Sala BeCool
A favourite in the chic Sant Gervasi neighbourhood, Sala BeCool offers a wide-ranging programme of DJ sessions, club nights and live gigs. ✆ Plaça Joan Llongueras 5 • Map C1

Otto Zutz
Barcelona's media crowd flocks to this New-York-style club to chatter in the corners upstairs and shoot pool downstairs. The huge dance floors throb with house music. ✆ C/Lincoln 15 • Closed Sun • Adm

La Cervesera Artesana
This friendly micro-brewery offers a good range of imported beers in addition to their own excellent brews. The Iberian Pale Ale, a mellow amber beer, is well worth a try. ✆ C/Sant Agustí 14 • Map F1 • Open from 6pm daily

Heliogàbal
This cult live music venue is best on Thursday or Sunday nights when you can hear anything from an indie band to a poetry slam. Prices are very reasonable too. ✆ C/Ramón y Cajal 80 • Map F1 • Closed Mon

Bikini
Open from midnight, this huge venue has three spaces, which offer dance and Latin music and a cocktail lounge. Regular live music includes some of the best acts in Europe. ✆ Av Diagonal 547 • Closed Sun–Wed • Adm • DA

Around Town – Gràcia,Tibidabo & Zona Alta

Normal closing times for bars is 2:30am, 3am weekends. Clubs open until 4:30/5am. For more on Barcelona's nightlife See pp46–7

Price Categories

For a three-course meal for one with half a bottle of wine (or equivalent meal), taxes and extra charges.	**€** under €15
	€€ €15–25
	€€€ €25–35
	€€€€ €35–45
	€€€€€ over €45

Hofmann

10 Restaurants & Tapas Bars

1 El Asador d'Aranda
Housed in the magnificent *Modernista* Casa Roviralta, this restaurant is a magnet for business-folk. Order the delicious lamb roasted in an oak-burning oven and dine in the beautiful garden. ✪ *Av Tibidabo 31 • 93 417 01 15 • Closed Sun dinner • €€€€*

2 Acontraluz
This restaurant in a quiet part of town has a charming terrace and a retractable roof for alfresco dining in the summer. On the menu is modern Catalan cuisine, plus a range of tapas. ✪ *C/Milanesat 19 • 93 203 06 58 • €€€€*

3 Hofmann
Run by talented chef Mey Hofmann, this restaurant serves delicious Catalan cuisine. Save room for the exceptional desserts. ✪ *C/La Granada del Penedès 14–16 • 93 218 71 65 • Closed Sat, Sun, Easter Week, Aug, Christmas • DA • €€€€€*

4 Neichel
Top-class in every way, Neichel lures a moneyed clientele with *nouvelle cuisine*, but there is a €40 *petit menu*, too. Reserve in advance. ✪ *C/Beltrán i Rózpide 1 • 93 203 84 08 • Closed Sun, Mon, 3 weeks Aug • DA • €€€€€*

5 Abissínia
At this Ethiopian restaurant delicious sauces are served with *injera* bread. A good option for vegetarians. ✪ *C/Torrent de les Flors 55 • 93 213 70 85 • Closed Tue • €€*

6 Il Giardinetto
This eatery serves elaborate Mediterranean dishes such as spaghetti alla Sofia Loren (pasta with anchovy and parsley sauce). Piano music on Fridays. ✪ *C/La Granada del Penedès 28 • Map E1 • 93 218 75 36 • Closed Sat lunch, Sun, Aug • €€€€*

7 Fragments Café
Plaça de la Concòrdia, in the Les Corts neighbourhood, still retains a small-town appeal. This sweet little café serves delicious gourmet tapas out on the terrace or in the cosy interior. ✪ *Plaça de la Concòrdia 12 • 93 321 09 44 • €€*

8 La Balsa
In the quiet Bonanova district, La Balsa is a beautiful spot, with two garden terraces. Fine Basque, Catalan and Mediterranean dishes are served. ✪ *C/Infanta Isabel 4 • 93 211 50 48 • Closed Sun dinner, Mon lunch, Easter, lunch in Aug • €€€€€*

9 El Vell Sarrià
Housed in a handsome old town house, this is the best place in the area to try delicious paellas, local rice dishes and grilled seafood. ✪ *C/Major de Sarrià 93 • 93 204 57 10 • Closed Sun dinner, Mon • €€€€€*

10 Botafumeiro
The fish tanks at this seafood restaurant are teeming with crabs and lobster destined for plates. Try the tender *pulpo Gallego* (Galician octopus). Reservations are essential. ✪ *C/Gran de Gràcia 81 • 93 218 42 30 • DA • €€€€€*

Unless otherwise stated, all restaurants accept credit cards. For more on dining and standard opening hours **See p138**

117

Left **Monestir de Santes Creus** Right **Cadaqués**

Beyond Barcelona

*S*TEEPED IN TRADITION, *with its own language and an enormous sense of pride in its separate identity, Catalonia is immensely rich in both cultural heritage and physical geography. It is no exaggeration to say that Catalonia really does have everything. To the north are the 3,000-m (9840-ft) peaks of the Pyrenees. The coastline is dotted with hundreds of beautiful sandy beaches and intimate rocky coves with crystal-clear waters. These staggering natural treasures are complemented by a wealth of fabulous churches and monasteries, many set in stunning, isolated mountain scenery. For the gourmet, the regional cuisine is particularly rewarding, while the locally produced cava easily holds its own against its French champagne counterparts.*

Teatre-Museu Dalí

TOP 10 Sights & Attractions

1. Montserrat
2. Teatre-Museu Dalí, Figueres
3. Vall de Núria
4. Alt Penedès
5. Begur & Around
6. Tarragona
7. Girona
8. Empúries
9. Port Aventura
10. Costa Daurada & Sitges

Map of Catalonia showing:

FRANCE

ANDORRA

ARAGON

CATALUNYA

Vielha, Bol-Taüll, Sort, La Seu d'Urgell, Parc Nacional d'Aigüestortes i Estany de Sant Maurici, Puigcerdà, Martinet, Serra de l'Albera, Cap de Creus, **3 Vall de Núria**, Ribes de Freser, Sant Joan de les Abadesses, Figueres **2**, Roses, Cadaqués, Parc Natural del Cadí Moixeró, Massís de Pedraforca, Tremp, Ripoll, N260, Empúries **8**, Parc Natural dels Aiguamolls de l'Empordà, Parc Natural de la Zona Volcànica de la Garrotxa, l'Escala, l'Estartit, **7 Girona**, **5 Begur**, Solsona, Vic, Santa Cristina d'Aro, Platja d'Aro, Balaguer, Parc Natural de Sant Llorenç del Munt, Parc Natural del Montseny, Sant Feliu de Guíxols, Tossa de Mar, Lleida, Cervera, Manresa, Granollers, Terrassa, Sant Celoni, Blanes, Tàrrega, **Montserrat 1**, Igualada, Sabadell, Calella, Mataró, Santa Coloma de Gramanet, **Alt Penedès 4**, Montblanc, S. Sadurní d'Anoia, **Barcelona**, L'Espluga de Francolí, A2 AP2 (E9), El Prat de Llobregat, Reus, **Tarragona 6**, **10** Sitges, Castelldefels, **Port Aventura 6**, Costa Daurada, Tortosa, Delta de l'Ebre, Mar Mediterrània

50 — miles ─ 0 ─ km — 50

For tips on getting around Catalonia See p132

1 Montserrat

The dramatic mount of Montserrat, with its remote Benedictine monastery (dating from 1025), is a religious symbol and a place of pilgrimage for the Catalan people. The Basilica houses a statue of Catalonia's patron virgin, La Moreneta, also know as the "Black Virgin". Some legends date the statue to AD 50, but research

Basilica, Monestir de Montserrat

suggests it was carved in the 12th century. The monastery was largely destroyed in 1811 during the War of Independence, and rebuilt some 30 years later. Montserrat forms part of a ridge of mountains that rise suddenly from the plains. Take the funicular to the mountain's unspoilt peaks, where paths run alongside spectacular gorges to numerous hermitages. ◈ Tourist Info: Pl de la Creu • 93 877 77 01 • www.montserratvisita.com

2 Teatre-Museu Dalí, Figueres

Salvador Dalí was born in the town of Figueres in 1904. Paying tribute to the artist is the fantastic Teatre-Museu Dalí, which is full of his eccentric works. Housed in a former theatre, the country's second-most-visited museum (after the Prado in Madrid) provides a unique insight into the artist's extraordinary creations, from La Cesta de Pan (1926) to El Torero Alucinogeno (1970). A 30-minute drive away, near the beach town of Cadaqués, the Dalí connection continues. Here you can visit the Casa-Museu Salvador Dalí, the artist's summer house for nearly 60 years until his death in 1989.

◈ Pl Gala-Salvador Dalí, Figueres • 97 267 75 00 • Open Mar–Jun, Oct: 9:30am–6pm Tue–Sun (daily in Jun); Jul–Sep: 9am–8pm (Aug: midnight) daily; Nov–Feb: 10:30am–6pm Tue–Sun • Adm
◈ Casa-Museu Salvador Dalí, Portlligat, Cadaqués • 97 225 10 15 • Closed early Jan to mid-Feb • Guided visits only, Tue–Sun (15 Jun–15 Sep daily) by reservation • Adm • www.salvador-dali.org

3 Vall de Núria

This enchanting Pyrenean hideaway, surrounded by crests reaching as high as 3,000-m (9,840-ft), is a ski resort in winter and attracts hikers and nature-lovers in summer. The mountain resort is a religious sanctuary and has a youth hostel and apartments for rent. The valley is only accessible via a silent cog railway, which trundles above the clouds through breathtaking scenery. ◈ Tourist Info: Railway Station, Vall de Núria • 97 273 20 20 • Rack railway train from Ribes de Freser, 10 km N Ripoll

Rainy Taxi, Teatre-Museu Dalí

Anywhere in Catalonia can be reached by car from Barcelona in less than three hours.

4 Alt Penedès

Catalonia's most famous wine region is the *cava*-producing area of the Penedès. The *cava* brands of Cordoníu and Freixenet have become household names worldwide. Many of the area's wineries and bodegas are open to the public. One of the most spectacular is the Cordoníu bodega, housed in a *Modernista* building designed by Puig i Cadafalch, with a phenomenal 26 km (16 miles) of cellars on five floors. ✪ *Tourist Info: C/Cort 14, Vilafranca del Penedès • 93 818 12 54 • Contact the tourist office for details on all winery visits in the region • www.turismevilafranca.cat*

5 Begur & Around

The elegant hilltop town of Begur, with its ruined 14th-century castle, looks down over pristine wetlands and some of the prettiest coves on the Costa Brava. The town's population quadruples in summer as visitors make this their base for exploring nearby beaches and small, isolated coves. Many of the area's beaches stage jazz concerts throughout the summer. This is perhaps the best stretch of coastline in Catalonia. ✪ *Tourist Info: Av Onze de Setembre 5 • 97 262 45 20 • www.begur.cat*

6 Tarragona

Now a huge industrial port, Tarragona was once the capital of Roman Catalonia, and the city's main attractions today are from this era. Archaeological treasures include an impressive amphitheatre and the well-kept Roman walls that lead past the Museu Nacional Arqueològic and the Torre de Pilatos, a tower where Christians were

Riu Onyar, Girona

supposedly imprisoned before being thrown to the lions. Also in Tarragona is the Catedral de Santa Tecla *(see p124)*. ✪ *Tourist Info: C/Major 39 • 97 725 07 95 • www.tarragonaturisme.cat*

7 Girona

Said to have the highest living standards in Catalonia, Girona is a beautiful town surrounded by lush green hills. Hidden away in the old town, the atmospheric Jewish quarter (known as El Call) is one of the best- preserved medieval enclaves in Europe. Girona's cathedral is a must *(see p124)*. ✪ *Tourist Info: C/Joan Maragall 2 • 87 297 59 75 • www.girona.cat/turisme*

8 Empúries

After Tarragona, Empúries is Catalonia's second most important Roman site. Occupying an impressive position by the sea, it includes more than 40 hectares (99 acres) scattered with Greek and Roman ruins, the highlights of which are the remains of a market street, various temples and part of a Roman amphitheatre. Coupled with lovely nearby beaches, it's an ideal spot for those looking to mix a bit of history with a dip in the sea. ✪ *C/Puig i Cadafalch s/n, Empúries • 97 277 02 08 • Open*

Codorníu *cava*

Jun–Sep, Easter: 10am–8pm daily; Oct–May: 10am–6pm daily • Adm (free last Sun of month)

Port Aventura

Universal Studios' theme park is divided up into five areas: China, Far West, Mediterranean, Polynesia and Mexico, each offering rides and attractions. Thrill-junkies will appreciate one of Europe's biggest roller coasters, Dragon Kahn (China). There are also shows, and the entire experience is like being on a film set. ◎ Av Pere Molas, Vila-seca, Tarragona • 902 20 22 20 • Open Apr–Oct & Christmas daily, Nov–Mar Sat & Sun; call for seasonal hours • Adm • DA

Costa Daurada & Sitges

With its wide sandy beaches and shallow waters, the Costa Daurada differs from the northern Catalonian coastline. The sleepy town of Torredembarra is a pleasant and rarely busy family resort, but the jewel in the crown is undoubtedly Sitges. It's the summer home to Barcelona's chic crowd, as well as being a popular gay resort (see p49). Despite its cosmopolitan, frenetic feel, the town never reaches the tacky excesses of some of the Costa Brava's resorts. ◎ Tourist Info: Plaça Eduard Maristany 2, Sitges • 93 894 42 51 • www.sitgestur.cat

Waterfront, Sitges

A Scenic Drive

Morning

From Barcelona take the AP7 motorway until exit 4, then take the C260 to Cadaqués. The journey should take about two and a half hours in all. Just before dropping down to the town, stop at the viewpoint and take in the azure coastline and the whitewashed houses of this former fishing village. Once in **Cadaqués**, now one of Catalonia's trendiest beach towns, wander the quaint boutique-filled streets. After a splash in the sea and a coffee on one of the chic terrace cafés, take the road leaving Port Lligat and head for the **Cap de Creus** (see p125) lighthouse. Drive through the desolately beautiful landscape of this rocky headland before doubling back and heading off to Port de la Selva. The road twists and winds interminably, but the picture-perfect scenery will leave you speechless.

Afternoon

Stop in the tiny, mountain-enclosed Port de la Selva for an excellent seafood lunch at **Ca l'Herminda**. Then drive to the neighbouring village of Selva del Mar with its tiny river and have a post-prandial coffee on the terrace of the Bar Stop before continuing up to the **Monestir Sant Pere de Rodes** (see p124). You'll be tempted to stop several times on the way up to take in the views. Don't, because the best is to be had from the monastery, which offers an incredible sweeping vista of the whole area. There are plenty of well-signposted walks around the mountain top here and it is worth staying put to see the sun set slowly over the bay.

Following pages **Inner Courtyard, Monestir de Montserrat**

121

Left **Chapterhouse detail, Monestir de Santes Creus** Right **Monestir de Poblet**

🔟 Churches & Monasteries

1 Monestir de Montserrat

Catalonia's holiest place is the region's most visited monastery. It boasts some Romanesque art and a statue of the "Black Virgin" (see p119). ◉ Montserrat • 93 877 77 01 • Adm (to museums); free (to basilica) • DA to basilica

2 Monestir de Poblet

This busy, working monastery contains the Gothic Capella de Sant Jordi, a Romanesque church, and the Porta Daurada, a doorway that was gilded for Felipe II's visit in 1564. ◉ off N240, 10 km W of Montblanc • 97 787 02 54 • Adm

3 Monestir de Ripoll

The west portal of this monastery (879) has reputedly the finest Romanesque carvings in Spain. Of the original buildings, only the doorway and cloister remain. ◉ Ripoll • 97 270 23 51 • Adm

4 Monestir de Santes Creus

The cloister at this Gothic treasure (1150) is notable for the beautifully sculpted capitals by English artist Reinard Funoll. ◉ Santes Creus, 25 km NW of Montblanc • 97 763 83 29 • Closed Mon • Adm

5 Monestir de Sant Pere de Rodes

The dilapidated charm of this UNESCO World Heritage Site may have dwindled since its face-lift, but the views it offers over Cap de Creus and Port de la Selva are still breathtaking. ◉ 22 km E of Figueres • 97 238 75 59 • Closed Mon • Adm

6 Sant Climent i Santa Maria de Taüll

These two churches are perfect examples of the Romanesque churches that pepper the Pyrenees. Dating from 1123, most of the original frescoes are now in the MNAC in Barcelona (see pp18–19). ◉ 138 km N of Lleida • 97 369 67 15 • www.centreromanic.com

7 Catedral de La Seu d'Urgel

Dating from around 1040, this cathedral is one of the most elegant in Catalonia. ◉ La Seu d'Urgell • 97 335 32 42 • Adm • DA

8 Catedral de Santa Maria

This cathedral possesses the widest Gothic nave anywhere in Europe and the second widest of any type after the Basilica in the Vatican. ◉ Old Town, Girona • 97 222 65 75 • Adm • Sun free

9 Catedral de Santa Tecla

At 104-m (340-ft) long, Tarragona's cathedral is the largest in the region. Its architecture is a mixture of Gothic and Romanesque, and it is crowned by a huge octagonal bell tower. ◉ Old Town, Tarragona • 97 722 69 35 • Closed Sun • Adm • Guided tours

10 Sant Joan de les Abadesses

This pretty French Romanesque-style monastery in the Pyrenees harbours a prestigious collection of Romanesque sculpture. ◉ Sant Joan de les Abadesses • 97 272 23 53 • www.santjoandelesabadesses.com • Adm

 Usual opening hours for monasteries and churches are 10am–1pm & 3–7pm Mon–Sat, 10am–1pm Sun. Call to confirm seasonal times.

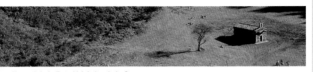

Parc Natural de la Zona Volcànica de la Garrotxa

🔟 National Parks & Nature Reserves

1 Parc Nacional d'Aigüestortes i Estany de Sant Maurici
The magnificent peaks of Catalonia's only national park are accessible from the resort of Espot. You'll find ponds and lakes 2,000 m (6,560 ft) up. 🧭 *148 km N of Lleida*

2 Delta de l'Ebre
This giant delta is a patchwork of paddy fields. The wide expanse of the River Ebre is a nature reserve for migratory birds and has scores of bird-watching stations. 🧭 *28 km SE of Tortosa*

3 Parc Natural de la Zona Volcànica de la Garrotxa
It is 10,000 years since La Garrotxa last erupted and the volcanoes are long since extinct. The largest crater is the Santa Margalida, at 500 m (1,640 ft) wide. It is magical here in spring when thousands of butterflies emerge. 🧭 *40 km NW of Girona*

4 Cap de Creus
As the Pyrenees tumble into the Mediterranean, they create a rocky headland, which juts out 10 km (6.25 miles). It forms Catalonia's most easterly point and offers spectacular views of the craggy coastline. 🧭 *36 km E of Figueres*

5 Parc Natural del Cadí-Moixeró
Covered in a carpet of conifers and oaks, this mountain range has surprisingly lush vegetation. Several peaks are over 2,000 m (6,560 ft) high. 🧭 *20 km E of La Seu d'Urgell*

6 Parc Natural del Montseny
Forming Catalonia's most accessible natural park, these woodland hills are well-equipped for walkers and mountain bikers, with a huge network of trails. Climb the well-signposted and popular Turó de l'Home, which is the highest peak. 🧭 *48 km NW of Barcelona*

7 Massís de Pedraforca
A nature reserve surrounds this huge outcrop of mountains, a favourite of rock climbers with peaks rising to 2,500 m (8,200 ft). 🧭 *64 km N of Manresa*

8 Serra de l'Albera
On the eastern part of the border between Spain and France, the tree-covered slopes of Albera are speckled with interesting ruins. 🧭 *15 km N of Figueres*

9 Parc Natural dels Aiguamolls de l'Empordà
This nature reserve hides bird-watching towers. Those in the Laguna de Vilalt and La Bassa de Gall Mari allow bird-lovers to observe herons, moorhens and other bird species nesting in spring. 🧭 *15 km E of Figueres*

10 Parc Natural de Sant Llorenç del Munt
Surrounded by industry and within easy reach of Barcelona, this is a surprisingly untamed park inhabited by large numbers of wild boar. Walk up Cerro de la Mola to see the Romanesque monastery. 🧭 *12 km E of Manresa*

Rafting, La Noguera Pallaresa

Outdoor Activities

Rafting & Kayaking
One of Europe's best rivers for white-water sports is La Noguera Pallaresa in the Pyrenees. Late spring is the best time to go, as the mountain snow thaws.
ⓢ *Yeti Emotions, Llavorsí, 14 km N of Sort • 97 362 22 01 • www.yetiemotions.com*

Scuba Diving
Reserva Natural de les Illes Medes has thousands of species and coral reefs. Glassbottomed boats cater to non-divers.
ⓢ *Aquàtica, L'Estartit • 97 275 06 56 • www.aquatica-sub.com*

Watersports & Sailing
Good sailing can be found in Sitges, along with yachts for rent, classes for the novice, canoeing and windsurfing. ⓢ *La Club de Mar Sitges, Pg Marítim, Sitges • 93 894 09 05 • http://clubdemardesitges.com*

Skiing
La Molina is the most accessible Pyrenean ski-resort from Barcelona, but Baqueira-Beret is where the jet-set goes. Both offer all levels of skiing (including off-piste) from December. ⓢ *La Molina, 25 km S of Puigcerdà • 972 89 20 31 • www.lamolina.com • Baqueira-Beret, 14 km E of Vielha • 902 415 415 • www.baqueira.cat*

Golf
The Costa Brava is one of Europe's top golf destinations; the best courses are around Platja d'Aro. ⓢ *Santa Cristina d'Aro • 972 83 70 55* ⓢ *Platja d'Aro • 97 281 67 27*

Horse Riding
Montseny National Park *(see p125)* is ideal for horse riding, with a number of centres. ⓢ *Can Marc, 6 km W of Sant Celoni • Closed Mon • 93 848 27 13*

Ballooning
A balloon journey over the volcanic area of La Garrotxa is an unbeatable way to get a bird's-eye view of Catalonia. ⓢ *Vol de Coloms • 97 268 02 55, or 68 9471 872 • www.voldecoloms.cat*

Boat trips
Take a cruise from Calella and Blanes to Tossa de Mar, stopping at the old town and the castle of Tossa de Mar. ⓢ *Dofi Jet Boats, Blanes • 97 235 20 21 www.dofi-jetboats.com • boats every hour daily from Blanes and Lloret de Mar (twice daily from Calella) • Closed Nov–Mar*

Windsurfing, Rowing & Golf
Used for rowing competitions in the 1992 Olympics, the huge Canal Olímpic is now a leisure complex offering a host of activities. ⓢ *Canal Olímpic • Av Canal Olímpic, Castelldefels • 93 636 28 96 • www.canalolimpic.com*

Foraging for Mushrooms
From late September to late October, thousands of Catalans flock to the hills in search of the highly prized *rovelló*. There are also poisonous varieties, so amateurs should get a guide through the Diputació de Barcelona.

Diputació de Barcelona has information on activities in Catalonia, from gastro tours to guided walks. www.catalunya.com

Price Categories

For a three-course	**€**	under €15
meal for one with half	**€€**	€15–25
a bottle of wine (or	**€€€**	€25–35
equivalent meal), taxes	**€€€€**	€35–45
and extra charges.	**€€€€€**	over €45

Anchovy tapas, El Pescadors

TOP 10 Places to Eat

1 El Taller
A historic townhouse in Tossa de Mar's walled old town houses this charming restaurant offering fine Mediterranean seafood and meat dishes. ◈ *C/Pou de la Vila 9, Tossa de Mar • 97 234 03 26 • Closed Sun eve, Mon & Tue in winter* • €€€

2 El Racó de Can Fabes
Celebrated late chef Santi Santamaria has been succeeded by Xavier Pellicer, but his philosophy – sublime food made with the finest local ingredients – lives on at this award-winning restaurant. ◈ *Sant Joan 6, Sant Celoni, Montseny • 93 867 28 51 • Closed Sun eve, Mon, Tue • DA* • €€€€€

3 La Torre del Remei
A *Modernista* palace provides an elegant setting for wonderfully presented Catalan food. ◈ *Camí del Remei 3, Bolvir, Cerdanya, 3 km SW of Puigcerdà • 97 214 01 82 • DA* • €€€€€

4 El Mirador de les Caves
This restaurant is set in a castle overlooking Catalonia's wine country. Traditional cuisine is complemented by bottles of local wine and *cava*. ◈ *Els Casots, 4 km S of Sant Sadurní d'Anoia • 93 899 31 78 • Closed Sun & Mon eves* • €€€€€

5 Fonda Europa
Established in 1771, Fonda Europa was the first in a line of successful Catalan restaurants. Ample portions include pig's trotters. ◈ *C/Anselm Clavé 1, Granollers • 93 870 03 12 • DA* • €€€

6 L'Angle
The modern interior of this Michelin-starred restaurant is the ideal setting for contemporary cuisine prepared with fresh local produce. ◈ *Hotel Món, Camí de Sant Benet de Bages, Sant Fruitós de Bages • 93 875 94 29 • Closed Mon–Wed, Thu & Sun eves* • €€€€€

7 Carme Ruscalleda Sant Pau
Carme Ruscalleda is said to be one of the finest chefs in the country. Her restaurant in this seaside village offers sublime Catalan cuisine. ◈ *C/Nou 10, Sant Pol de Mar • 93 760 06 62 • Closed Sun, Mon, Thu lunch, 3 wks May, 3 wks Nov* • €€€€€

8 Els Pescadors
"The Fishermen", a traditional *Empordà*-style restaurant, offers local specialities, including an array of blue fish dishes. ◈ *Port d'en Perris 3, l'Escala • 97 277 07 28 • Closed Sun eve & Thu (winter) & Nov* • €€€€

9 El Celler de Can Roca
The Roca brothers' exciting, contemporary Catalan cuisine is complemented by a great choice of wines. There is a ten-month waiting list! ◈ *C/Can Sunyer 48, Girona • 97 222 21 57 • Closed Sun, Mon, Easter Week, 3 wks in Dec–Jan* • €€€€€

10 Cal Ton
Contemporary cuisine in the heart of Catalonia's biggest wine region. Try the *menu degustació*. ◈ *C/Casal 8, Vilafranca del Penedès • 93 890 37 41 • Closed Mon, Sun eve, Easter, 3 wks in Aug* • €€€€€

Unless otherwise stated, all restaurants accept credit cards.
For more on dining and standard opening hours **See p138**

STREETSMART

BARCELONA'S TOP 10

Left **Airport sign** Right **Iberia logo**

Tips on Getting To Barcelona

By Air
British Airways, Iberia and Vueling offer direct flights from the UK; there are also low-cost airlines like Ryanair and easyJet. From the US, United and Delta fly direct from NY and Atlanta. Qantas flies to Barcelona from Australia and New Zealand via a series of stopovers. ✈ *British Airways: 902 111 333 • www.britishairways.com* ✈ *Iberia: 902 400 500 • www.iberia.es* ✈ *Vueling: 807 200 100 • www.vueling.com* ✈ *Ryanair: www.ryanair.com* ✈ *easyJet: 902 599 900 (premium rate) • www.easyjet.com* ✈ *Delta: 902 810 872 • www.delta.com*

Barcelona Airport
Prat de Llobregat airport's two terminals are 12 km (7 miles) south of the city centre. They are linked by a shuttle bus. ✈ *902 404 704 • www.aena.es*

From the Airport
The Aerobús links the airport to the city centre; it departs every 6 minutes (6am–1am) and makes various stops, terminating at Plaça de Catalunya. There are two Aerobús lines, A1 and A2 (one for each terminal). RENFE trains leave the airport every half hour, stopping at Estació de Sants and Passeig de Gràcia; both link up with the metro. A taxi into the city centre costs €25–35. ✈ *Aerobús: 902 100 104 • www.aerobusbcn.com* ✈ *RENFE: 902 320 320 • www.renfe.es*

By Train
Trains run throughout Spain and Europe from Estació de Sants and Estació de França. Sants has several services, including lockers, ATMs and bureaux de change, but França has none. RENFE is Spain's national train company. ✈ *Estació de França, Av Marquès de l'Argentera • Map Q5* ✈ *Estació de Sants, Pl dels Països Catalans • Off map* ✈ *RENFE: 902 320 320 (24 hours) • www.renfe.es*

By Bus
Both Eurolines and Movelia serve Barcelona from numerous European cities, including Rome, Paris and London. Buses usually operate from Barcelona's Estació del Nord and Estació de Sants. ✈ *Estació del Nord, C/Ali Bei 80 • Map R2 • 902 26 06 06 • www.barcelonanord.com* ✈ *Eurolines: 902 40 50 40 • www.eurolines.com* ✈ *Movelia: 902 33 55 33 • www.movelia.com*

By Car
Barcelona is linked to the rest of Spain and Europe by *autopistes* (toll highways) and toll-free roads. The tolled AP7 runs between Barcelona and the border of France.

Domestic travel
The city is connected to the rest of Spain by train, bus and plane. Iberia flies to and from many domestic destinations and offer a shuttle service between Madrid and Barcelona with up to 30 flights a day. Vueling and Air Europa serve Barcelona from the rest of Spain. The fast AVE train service connects Barcelona to Madrid. RENFE and several bus companies link Barcelona to most of Spain's major cities. ✈ *Air Europa: 902 40 15 01 • www.aireuropa.com*

Cheap Travel
Book long before your departure date to cut costs. If you're flexible, you're likely to find better deals. The Internet is great for cheap fares (try www.kayak.co.uk or www.travelocity.com). Many airlines offer discounts if you buy online.

Planning
Citizens from the US, Canada, the UK, Ireland, Australia and New Zealand need a valid passport. Non-EU citizens need a visa if they intend to stay in Spain for longer than three months. Always check the latest requirements with the Spanish embassy in your country before leaving. If you're taking any kind of medication, bring your prescription.

When to Visit
If you're in search of sun, visit Barcelona in the summer, but be aware that many businesses close through August. To avoid the crowds, visit around May or October.

Left **Metro sign** Centre **Barcelona taxi** Right **Tram**

🔟 Tips on Getting Around Barcelona

1 Metro

Barcelona's 11-line metro system is convenient, fast, easy to use and extensive. The metro stays open all night on Saturdays. ✆ 902 07 50 27 • www.tmb.cat • Open 5am–midnight Mon–Thu, 5am–2am Fri, 5am Sat–midnight Sun

2 FGC

The FGC (Ferrocarrils de la Generalitat de Catalunya) is the city's commuter rail system, serving northern and eastern Barcelona. The FGC shares several key stations with the metro, including Plaça de Catalunya and Plaça d'Espanya, and has the same prices and similar hours. ✆ 93 205 15 15 • www.fgc.cat • Open 5am–midnight Mon–Thu, 5am–2am Fri–Sat, 6am–midnight Sun

3 Bus

Barcelona's bus system covers the entire city. Bus stops are clearly marked and buses have their destinations on the front. For information on routes and schedules call 010 or pick up a bus guide from tourist offices. ✆ 902 07 50 27 • www.tmb.cat • 6am–10:30pm daily

4 Nightbus

There are about 17 Nitbús (nightbus) routes across the city, many of which pass through Plaça de Catalunya. ✆ 93 223 51 51 • www.emt-amb.com

5 Tickets & Passes

A single fare on the metro, FGC, bus or night-bus costs €2. The T-10 personal ticket (€9.25) permits 10 journeys on metro, FGC and bus, as long as the total journey is completed within 75 minutes. There are also one-, two-, three-, four- and five-day passes that provide unlimited travel on public transport. Tickets can be bought from machines at all metro stations.

6 Taxi

Hail a yellow-and-black taxi on any major street in town; a green light on the roof indicates that one is free. For two or more passengers, taxis are almost as cheap as the metro for short hops. A minimum fare applies. ✆ Radio Taxi: 93 303 30 33 ✆ Barna Taxi: 93 322 22 22

7 On Foot

Barcelona is extremely compact and most areas are best negotiated on foot, especially the old town and Gràcia, where a leisurely stroll is the only way to soak up the architectural and cultural riches. Barcelona's waterfront, from the Port Vell to the Port Olímpic, is also made for walking. See pp58–9.

8 By Bicycle

Pedalling around the port, Barri Gòtic or Parc de la Ciutadella is a fun alternative to walking. There are over 180 km (112 miles) of bike lanes throughout the city, outlined on maps available from the tourist office and bike rental shops. Bikes are available to rent daily from Budget Bikes or Barcelona by Bicycle. Barcelona Battery Bikes has electric bikes. ✆ Budget Bikes: 93 304 18 85 • www.budgetbikes.eu ✆ Barcelona by Bicycle: 93 268 21 05 • www.bicicleta barcelona.com ✆ www. barcelonabatterybikes.com

9 Transport for the Disabled

The airport bus is accessible to wheelchair users as are Lines 2, 9, 10 and 11 of the metro, all city buses and nightbuses, a few FGC stations and the Montjuïc cable car. Taxi Amic has cars and vans dedicated to wheelchair users – call in advance. For information on transport for the disabled, call Institut Municipal de Persones amb Discapacitat (IMD). For details on specific routes, call 010 or check the TMB website. ✆ Taxi Amic: 93 420 80 88 • IMD: 93 413 27 75 ✆ TMB: 90 207 50 27 • www.tmb.cat

10 Getting Around in a Wheelchair

The IMPD (see p134) has a database that charts all the streets accessible to wheelchair users. Call 010, give your departure point and destination, and they'll advise you of an accessible route.

Left **RENFE train ticket** Centre **Road sign** Right **RENFE sign**

📖10 Ways to Explore Catalonia

1 By Train
RENFE operates lines out of Barcelona in all directions, making it easy to escape the city. Most regional trains leave from Estació de Sants *(see p130)* and Estació Passeig de Gràcia. Call the RENFE information line for destinations and schedules. 🔊 *Estació Passeig de Gràcia • Pg de Gràcia • Map E2* 🔊 *RENFE • 902 320 320*

2 By Bus
Regional bus companies operate all over Catalonia. Most depart from Estació del Nord – call the station for information or check timetables online. 🔊 *Estació del Nord: C/Ali Bei 80 • Map R2 • 902 26 06 06 • www.barcelonanord.com*

3 By Car
A car is essential if you wish to explore off the beaten track, particularly in the Pyrenees and the Catalonian heartland. There are many car rental companies, including the big names (Avis, Budget, Hertz). All have offices at the airport. Prices range from €300–450 for a medium-sized car for a week. You must be over 25, and have a valid driver's licence, a credit card and a passport. Booking your rental car from abroad or online is often cheaper. 🔊 *Avis: 902 18 08 54 • www.avis.com* 🔊 *Budget: 902 11 25 85 • www.budget. com* 🔊 *Hertz: 902 40 24 05 • www.hertz.com*

4 By Bike
Mountain bikers will find a wealth of rugged terrain in the Pyrenees. The Turisme de Catalunya has maps and brochures, as well as a website showing regional bike routes. Terra Diversions offer a range of regional tours (including self-guided), and arrange bike rental. 🔊 *C/Santa Tecla 1 • 93 416 08 05 • www. terradiversions.com*

5 Sea Cruises
"Sightsea" off the Costa Brava aboard glass-bottomed boats and other sea cruisers. L'Aventura del Nautilus conducts coastal sea cruises from L'Estartit to the Medes Islands off the Costa Brava. Excursiones Marítimas plies the Mediterranean from Calella and Blanes to Tossa de Mar, stopping at lovely coves along the way. 🔊 *L'Aventura del Nautilus: L'Estartit, 100km N of Barcelona • 972 75 14 89* 🔊 *Dofí Jet Boats: Calella, 40 km N of Barcelona; Blanes, 60 km N of Barcelona • 972 35 20 21*

6 Bus Tours
Organized bus tours travel to the Monestir de Montserrat, Girona, the Teatre-Museu Dalí in Figueres and the Costa Brava. Also offered is a half-day tour of the wine and *cava* regions, and trips to Vic and Manresa, as well as hot-air balloon trips and bird-watching tours. Tours are organized by Barcelona tourist office, and can be booked online. Prices start at €65 for a full-day tour. 🔊 *Barcelona Tourism: 93 285 38 34 • www. barcelonaturisme.com*

7 Main Roads
Main roads are designated with an N (for *Nacional*) or C (for *Catalunya*). Road information is available at www.guiar epsol.com/es_en/home.

8 Avoiding Traffic
The best time to get out of town is in the late morning. Avoid long holiday weekends *(pont)* and Friday evenings, when traffic is always heavy. Since most Spanish take their holidays in August, motorways are particularly busy around this period.

9 Tips for Families
RENFE offers a 40 per cent discount for children aged four to 13; children under four who don't take up a seat travel free. Ask when booking tickets.

10 Turisme de Catalunya
This tourist office offers plenty of material on Catalonia, from maps to information on outdoor sports and festival listings. Changing exhibits on the region are also on display. 🔊 *Palau Robert, Pg de Gràcia 105 • Map E2 • 012 or 93 238 80 91 • www. gencat.cat/probert • Open 10am–7pm Mon–Sat, 10am–2:30pm Sun*

 For recommended trips out of Barcelona See pp118–27

Left **Las Golondrinas tour boat** Right **Bus Turístic, Plaça de Catalunya**

Tours & Trips

1 Bus Tours

The open-topped Bus Turístic has several routes. The red route explores northern Barcelona; the blue route takes in the southern area; and the green route (Apr–Sep only) travels along the beach front. A night tour is also available. You can hop on and off as many times as you like. Discounts to sights and shops are included. ⬡ Depart from Pl de Catalunya • Every 5–25 mins 9am–7pm (8pm Apr–Oct) daily • Purchase on the bus, at tourist offices or online at www.barcelona busturistic.cat

2 Walking Tours

The tourist office (see p134) organizes a selection of reasonably-priced guided walks from the main office in Plaça de Catalunya – these include tours of the Barri Gòtic, Modernista tours, seaside tours, gourmet tours and a Picasso-themed tour. The Travel Bar (see p134) also conducts lively walking tours.

3 La Ruta Modernista

The Modernisme Route guidebook contains several itineraries, a map and discount vouchers for all admission fees. For the guide, tours and information, visit the Centre del Modernisme at the Tourist Information Office in Plaça Catalunya. ⬡ 010 • www.rutadel modernisme.com

4 Boat Tours

See the city from the sea on one of Las Golondrinas' sightseeing boats. Trips lasting 35 minutes depart every half-hour; longer tours are available on a catamaran with an underwater view. Orsom operate catamaran and speedboat tours around the port. ⬡ Las Golondrinas: Portal de la Pau • 93 442 31 06 • www.las golondrinas.com ⬡ Orsom: Portal de la Pau • 93 441 05 37 • www.barcelona-orsom.com

5 Cable Cars

Cable cars (telefèric) depart from Montjuïc (Miramar station), Torre de Jaume I (currently closed for renovation) and Torre de Sant Sebastià, yielding stunning views of the city. ⬡ 93 441 48 20

6 Catalan Bird Tours

Let an English-speaking guide take you to some of the best birding sites in the region, including the Llobregat delta, near the airport. This surprisingly beautiful little nature reserve is a haven for resident and migratory birds. ⬡ 93 818 82 72 • www.catalanbirdtours.com

7 Helicopter Tours

Cat Helicopters offers three tours of Barcelona, which depart from their landing pad at the port. The 5-minute Costa Tour costs €45, and takes in the city coastline. For some of the city's biggest sights, including the Sagrada Familia, take the Skytour (10mins, €95); it can also be extended to Montserrat (35mins, €300). ⬡ Heliport, Passeig de l'Escullera, Moll Adossat • 93 224 07 10 • www. cathelicopters.com

8 Bike Tours

Whiz about the old town and the Parc de la Ciutadella on group bike tours organized by bike rental shops, such as Barcelona by Bicycle. Barcelona by Bike also runs bike tours in English. ⬡ Barcelona by Bicycle, C/Esparteria 3 • 93 268 21 05 • www.bicicleta barcelona.com ⬡ Barcelona by Bike: 93 268 81 07 • Open all year • www. barcelonabybike.com

9 Horse-drawn Carriages

It may be a tourist trap, but riding up La Rambla on a horse and carriage can raise a smile, especially for kids. ⬡ Depart from Pl de Portal de la Pau • 93 421 15 49

10 Go Car Tours

A cross between a two-person scooter and a small car, these tiny open-top vehicles are ideal for pottering between the sights of Barcelona. A helpful audio tour is included in the price. ⬡ 93 269 17 92 • www.gocartours.es

Left **Tourist information sign** Centre **Newsstand on La Rambla** Right **Tourist Information Centre**

Sources of Information

1 Tourist Information

Multilingual staff give out free maps and information at Barcelona's main tourist office on Plaça de Catalunya. They also have a hotel booking service, a bureau de change, Internet access and a souvenir shop. Other offices are located in Estació de Sants and on Plaça de Sant Jaume. For information on the rest of Catalonia, visit the Turisme de Catalunya *(see p132).* For information over the phone on everything from museum opening hours to bus routes, call 010 or the Turisme de Barcelona's information line. ◈ *Turisme de Barcelona, Pl de Catalunya 1 • Map M1 • 93 285 38 34 • Open 9am–9pm daily • www. barcelonaturisme.com*

2 Information Officers

In summer red-jacketed tourist information officers roam the city's busiest areas giving out maps and advice. There are also info points in Las Ramblas, Estació del Nord, Plaça Espanya, the airport and Sants train station.

3 Magazines

The weekly *Guía del Ocio* covers the city's nightlife (music, theatre, dance and film), has extensive restaurant listings and is available from all newsstands. *Barcelona Metropolitan* (free) is the city's leading English-language monthly

magazine, featuring culture, the arts and restaurant and nightlife listings. *b-guided* gives the latest on trendy places to shop, eat and drink – in English and Spanish.

4 Consulates

Various nations have consulates in Barcelona. ◈ *UK: Av Diagonal 477 • 902 109 356* ◈ *US: Pg Reina Elisenda 23 • 93 280 22 27* ◈ *Australia: Pl Gal.la Placidia 1–3, 1st floor • 93 490 90 13* ◈ *New Zealand: Travessera de Gràcia 64 • 93 209 03 99* ◈ *Canada: Plaça Catalunya 9 • 93 270 36 14* ◈ *Ireland: Gran Vía Carles III 94 • 93 491 50 21*

5 Institut de Cultura de Barcelona

Get the lowdown on cultural and arts events among others, from the Institut de Cultura in the Palau de la Virreina *(see p13).* ◈ *La Rambla 99 • 93 316 10 00 • Open 10am–8pm daily*

6 Websites

Numerous websites cover Barcelona, including the official tourist office site (www.barcelona turisme.com). Another excellent source is www. bcn.cat. The website of Turisme de Catalunya (www.catalunyaturisme. com) has extensive coverage of Catalonia.

7 Travel Bar

This friendly bar, with Internet access and amiable staff, is a good source of information.

The bar hosts guided walking *(see p133)* and bike tours, "intercambio" nights to practise your Spanish, and a popular bar crawl to the best bars of the old town. ◈ *C/Boqueria 27 • 93 342 52 52 • www. travelbar.com*

8 University Bulletins

If you're after cheap, short term accommodation or if you're looking to practise your Spanish, peruse the university notice boards posted around the building's cloisters. ◈ *Gran Via de les Corts Catalanes • 93 403 54 17*

9 Libraries & British Council

The city's main library is the Biblioteca de Catalunya; bring your passport to apply for a one-day pass. The British Council houses a library of English books and newspapers. ◈ *Biblioteca de Catalunya: C/Hospital 56 British Council: C/Amigó 83 • Closed Aug*

10 Disabled Travellers

Disabled access in Barcelona is limited, though getting better – especially in old buildings. The Institut Municipal de Persones amb Discapacitat (IMPD) provides a list of places with wheelchair access and can offer advice on getting around. ◈ *C/Valencia 344 • 93 413 27 75*

Left **Postage stamp** Centre **Telephone** Right **Mailbox**

TOP 10 Communication Tips

1 Public Phones
There are public phones (*cabines*) throughout the city. Use coins, a credit card or a phonecard.

2 Phonecards
Purchase a phonecard from a newsstand, phone centre or tobacco shop (*estanc*). The Telefónica phonecard comes in denominations of €5 and €10. Phone centres (*locutoris*) usually sell phone cards with a scratch-off pin number for cheap calls.

3 Long-Distance Calls
To make an international call, dial 00 followed by the country code (UK: 44; US/Canada: 1; Australia: 61; New Zealand: 64), the area code and the phone number. To call Spain from abroad, dial the international access code then 34 for Spain plus the full phone number. For operator assistance in making international calls from Spain, dial 11825. This is also the number to call if you want to make an international collect call as well as for international information and directory enquiries.

4 Local & Regional Calls
The cost of a local call from a phone booth to a land line is generally about 20 cents. Barcelona phone numbers all begin with the code 93; the rest of Catalonia is divided up into the provinces of Lleida (973), Girona (972) and Tarragona (977). For operator assistance, dial 11822.

5 Phone Centres
Phone centres (*locutoris*) provide a more comfortable – and usually cheaper – alternative to public pay phones. Phones are hooked up to a digital display showing the cost, which is paid at the end. You will find several in El Raval as well as around Sants station and in the Poble Sec neighbourhood.

6 Mobile Phones
Spain has several mobile phone operators, including Vodafone and Orange. Roaming rates vary widely, so check with your service provider before leaving.

7 Post
Post offices (*correus*) are usually open 8:30am–8:30pm Mon–Fri and 9:30am–1pm Sat, though hours may vary slightly. Barcelona's main post office is open longer hours. It also offers a range of services, including fax and express mail services (*urgente*). The city's mailboxes are bright yellow. ◈ *Main Post Office: Pl Antonio López • Open 8:30am–9:30pm Mon–Fri, 8:30am–2:30pm Sat*

8 Poste Restante
You can receive mail at any post office, but it's safest to have it sent to the main one. Bring your passport (or a copy of it) to collect mail. ◈ *Address letters to: Lista de Correos, 08080, Barcelona, Spain*

9 Internet Access
Internet centres are dotted all over Barcelona, many around Plaça de Catalunya and La Rambla. Most are open until 11pm, sometimes midnight. Phone centres (*locutoris*) usually also provide Internet access. The city council offers more than 180 Wi-Fi points around the city, including at parks and beaches, which allow free Internet for at least 1 hour (see *www.bcn.cat/barcelonawifi* for more information). Several cafés, hostels, hotels and bars offer Wi-Fi, although some charge for the service. ◈ *Workcenter: C/Roger de Lluria 2 (Plaça Urquinaona); Diagonal 923 (open 24 hours); Ronda Universitat 9 • www.workcenter.es*

10 Courier Services
Courier services will pick up a package and deliver it anywhere in the world, usually within 1–5 days. ◈ *Federal Express: 902 10 08 71* ◈ *UPS: 902 88 88 20* ◈ *DHL Worldwide Express: 902 12 24 24*

Left **Guardia Urbana** Centre **Pharmacy shop front** Right **Pharmacy sign**

Security & Health Tips

1 Emergencies

The national emergency number is 112, through which you can contact the *policia* (police), *bombers* (firemen) and *ambulància* (ambulance).

2 Police

Dial 091 to call the national police (Policia Nacional), and 092 for the local police (Guàrdia Urbana). If you need to report a crime, go to the nearest *comissaria*. ◎ *Comissaria, Old Centre: C/Nou de la Rambla 76–78 • 088 • Eixample: Via Laietana 43 • 93 290 33 23 • Also in Plaça de Catalunya train station (underground) • Open 24 hours*

3 Personal Security

Although petty crime is rife, more serious incidences of violence are rare. Thieves occasionally carry knives – if threatened, hand over your belongings immediately.

4 Valuables

Leave all your valuables, including your passport, behind in a hotel safety deposit box. Take as little cash as possible and carry what you do have in a money belt hidden under clothes. Carry wallets in front pockets and ensure bags are strapped across your front. On the beach and in cafés and restaurants, always keep your belongings on your lap or tied to your person. Also be cautious of any odd or unnecessary human contact, verbal or physical, whether it's a tap on the shoulder or someone spilling their drink at your table. Thieves often work in twos, so while one is catching your attention, the other is swiping your wallet.

5 Hospitals

Hospital Dos de Maig, Hospital de la Santa Creu i de Sant Pau *(see p103)* and Hospital Clinic all have 24-hour emergency rooms (called *urgències*). For an ambulance, dial 061. ◎ *Hospital Dos de Maig: C/Dos de Maig 301 • 93 507 27 00* ◎ *Hospital de la Santa Creu i de Sant Pau • C/Sant Antoni Maria Claret 167 • 93 291 90 00; 93 553 76 00 for emergencies* ◎ *Hospital Clinic: C/Villaroel 170 • 93 227 54 00*

6 Doctors & Clinics

The tourist office can provide information on English-speaking doctors. There are many walk-in clinics in the city (usually private), including the Creu Blanca near Plaça de Catalunya, where there is no need to make an appointment. There is also a 24-hour clinic at Passeig Reina Elisenda de Montcada, 17. ◎ *Creu Blanca: C/Pelai 40 • 93 412 12 12 • Open 8am–2pm, 4–8pm Mon–Sat*

7 Health Insurance

EU citizens can receive basic free medical care with a European health insurance card, which must be obtained before travelling. Non-EU citizens are strongly advised to take out medical cover.

8 Dental Treatment

Dental care is not covered by the EU health service. There are numerous dental clinics where you can walk in and get a consultation, including the Clínica Dental Barcelona, where dentists are generally on duty 9am–midnight daily. ◎ *Clínica Dental Barcelona: C/Pau Claris 194 • 93 487 83 29 • www. clinicadentalbarcelona.com*

9 Pharmacies

Pharmacies *(farmàcies)* are marked by a large green or red cross, usually in neon. All chemists have trained pharmacists who can offer advice (places on and around La Rambla usually have a pharmacist who speaks English). Regular hours are generally 10am–10pm. One pharmacy per neighbourhood is open all night from 9pm until 9am on a rotating basis (information is listed on the front door of each). Some pharmacies are open 24 hours, including the Farmacia Clapés (La Rambla 98).

10 Drinking Water

Spain's tap water is perfectly safe to drink. Most visitors, however, generally prefer to drink bottled water.

Left **La Caixa logo** Right **Twenty-euro note**

Banking & Money Tips

1 The Euro
Since January 2002, the official currency of Spain, and much of Europe, has been the Euro. For general information on the Euro check the European Union website.
⊗ http://ec.europa.eu

2 Banks
Banks are generally open 8am–2pm on week days. Some are open 4–8pm on Thursdays and 8am–2pm on Saturdays, except from July to September. Banks tend to offer better exchange and commission rates than bureaux de change, although rates do vary from bank to bank. There's a La Caixa exchange in Plaça de Catalunya, next to the tourist office, which stays open until 9pm. Numerous small bank branches exchange money in Estació de Sants train station and the airport; these are open from 7 or 8am to 10pm daily.

3 Changing Money
Avoid changing money at bureaux de change in tourist areas as commission rates tend to be high or exchange rates poor. On the whole, banks offer better deals, but bureaux de change have the advantage of longer opening hours. Some, particularly those on La Rambla, are open until midnight.

4 ATMs
ATMs (cash machines) provide the easiest way to access money and are a good way to beat commission charges. Surcharges depend on your bank. Relying on ATMs also means that you can take out money in smaller denominations and avoid carrying large amounts of cash. Before travelling, check with your bank that your PIN number works with foreign ATMs. All take VISA or MasterCard (Access) cards.

5 Travellers' Cheques
Buy travellers' cheques in Euros. All banks cash travellers' cheques, as do larger stores. Always carry the cheque numbers separately from the cheques. American Express and Thomas Cook are two well-known providers of travellers' cheques. Thomas Cook has also introduced "cash passport cards", which can be used at ATMs.

6 Credit Cards
Visa and MasterCard are readily accepted in all but budget hotels, restaurants and shops. American Express and Diner's Club cards are rarely accepted, except in the largest hotels and shops. Credit card cash advances are available from any bank (or ATM if you have a PIN number). Note that the transaction fee for cash advances on credit cards can be high.

7 Emergency Numbers
If your credit card is lost or stolen, call the police and your credit card company. Most credit cards have a number to call collect from abroad, which is provided at the time of issue. ⊗ Visa: 900 99 12 16 ⊗ MasterCard: 900 97 12 31 ⊗ American Express: 902 37 56 37

8 Online Banking
The quickest and cheapest way to keep track of your bank account and credit card bills is by checking them online. It's best to set up your online account before travelling.

9 Emergency Cash
It is advisable to carry some emergency cash hidden inside your luggage, separate from your wallet.

10 Tipping
Tipping is not the norm in Spain, though expectations are higher of tourists. Locals tip as follows: in restaurants, it is usually about five per cent of the bill. For a light meal, they round up the bill to the nearest 50 cents. Taxi drivers are usually tipped five per cent and hotel porters about 50 cents per bag.

Left **Coffee and croissant** Right **Terrace café, Barri Gòtic**

Eating & Drinking Tips

1 Opening Hours
The Spanish eat much later than much of Europe; lunch starts around 2 or 3pm, with dinner any time after 9pm. Restaurants are usually open 1:30–4pm and 8:30–midnight. Many are closed one day of the week and during the month of August. Cafés and bars are open from around 7:30am, closing around 2am. It is difficult to get a drink or bite to eat after 4am.

2 The Menu
Multilingual menus are increasingly the norm. Many restaurants offer their best deal for lunch from Monday to Friday, so do as the Spaniards do and fill up from the *menú del día* between 1:30 and 4pm. The fixed-price menu of the day usually includes three courses, wine and water.

3 Catalan Cuisine
Catalan cuisine is characterized by the meeting of *mar i muntanya* (surf and turf), and signature dishes include *llagosta i pollastre* (lobster and chicken). Side dish mainstays are *samfaina* (aubergine/ eggplant, grilled peppers, tomatoes and onion in olive oil and garlic) and *escalivada* (sweet peppers, aubergine, onion and garlic). Other Catalan favourites are *botifarra amb mongetes* (Catalan sausage with white beans) and *pa amb tomàquet* (bread smeared with tomato and drizzled with olive oil). If innards are your thing, ask for *call* (tripe). For dessert, enjoy *crema catalana*, a custard topped with caramelized sugar.

4 Seafood & Paella
For prime seafood, head for the sea. Along Passeig Joan de Borbó in Barceloneta is a string of restaurants, many specializing in seafood and paellas. Seafood restaurants also abound in the Port Olímpic, where you can feast on fresh-off-the-boat fish and seafood on open-air terraces. Fresh seafood is served year-round, but the traditional day for paella is Thursday.

5 Vegetarian
Barcelona has a handful of vegetarian eateries. Carrer Pintor Fortuny, in El Raval, has a couple of options, including Biocenter (at number 25), with its all-you-can-eat salad bar. Vegetarians can also feast almost anywhere on an array of tapas, including *patates braves* (spicy potatoes) and *truita de patates* (potato omelette). If you eat fish, then you'll be spoiled for choice.

6 Seasonal Specialities
From the end of the year until mid-Spring, try the Catalan speciality of *calçots*, sweet grilled scallions usually in a *romesco* sauce (spicy tomato sauce). Another autumn favourite are *bolets* (mushrooms), usually lightly grilled and served with a sprinkling of olive oil.

7 Etiquette
On 1 Jan 2011, smoking was banned in all public places, including bars and restaurants.

8 Tipping
Tipping is not expected in most establishments, so it's up to your own preference and how you rate the service. If leaving a tip, 5 per cent is usually acceptable. In upscale restaurants, however, a tip of 10 per cent is the norm. Catalans occasionally tip at the bar, perhaps leaving the small change from their drinks bill.

9 Children
The Spanish are relaxed about bringing children to restaurants and bars. Though kids' menus are rare, restaurants are often willing to serve half portions on request.

10 Disabled Access
All new restaurants must be wheelchair accessible by law, which includes access from the street to the dining room and at least one accessible bathroom. Contact the Institut Municipal de Persones amb Discapacitat *(see p134)* for a list of accessible restaurants. Always call ahead to check.

Left **Shopper, Pg de Gràcia** Centre **Shoe shop, C/Portaferrissa** Right **Clothes boutique, Gràcia**

⑩ Shopping Tips

1 Opening Hours

Most stores are open 10am to 2pm and 4:30pm to 8pm Monday to Saturday. Department stores and other large shops don't close at lunch time, and most stay open until 10pm.

2 Sales

Barcelona's big sales (rebaixes) come twice a year, from 1 July to the end of August and from 7 January until the end of February.

3 Reclaiming VAT

Non-EU citizens can claim an IVA (VAT) refund on most purchases over €90.15 when they leave Spain. Shops displaying the tax-free logo will provide a tax-refundable receipt, which you present before checking-in on departure. IVA (VAT) of 21 per cent (10 per cent on food) is included. IVA for hotels is 10 per cent, which is not always included in the price.

4 Leather

Leather items are a good buy in Spain and are of high quality. There are good shoe stores on C/ Portal de l'Àngel, C/Pelai, Rambla de Catalunya and Passeig de Gràcia. Loewe is famous for its quality leather goods. ✆ Loewe: Pg de Gràcia 35

5 Antiques

Antiques aficionados will be richly rewarded with a stroll along Carrer Banys Nous and Carrer de la Palla in the Barri Gòtic. For more antique finds, head to the Bulevard dels Antiquaris (see p50) on Passeig de Gràcia, home to over 60 antiques and arts shops. The antique markets, including the Mercat dels Antiquaris (see p53) and the Port Vell antique market, at weekends (10am–8pm), are also worth a browse.

6 Clothing

High-end clothing stores dot Passeig de Gràcia and Avinguda Diagonal. For trendier gear, head to Carrer Portaferrissa and Carrer Pelai. For the best original designs, check out the cool boutiques of La Ribera. Spain's success story is the wildly popular men's and women's contemporary clothing chain Zara, which is all over town (and the world). Another universal favourite is Mango, targeted towards younger women, which also has branches all over the city. If you're looking to buy local, there are a number of top-end Catalan designers, including Antonio Miró. ✆ Zara: Pg de Gràcia 16 ✆ Mango: Pg de Gràcia 65 ✆ Antonio Miró: C/Consell de Cent 349

7 Sizes

Clothing sizes tend to be small in Spain. Size conversions for women's clothing are: US/UK 6/8 is 36; 8/10 is 38; 10/12 is 40; 12/14 is 42; 14/16 is 44. For men's clothing, the conversions are: US & UK 36 is 46; 38 is 48; 40 is 50; 42 is 52.

8 Music

FNAC has a vast music selection, as does the department store El Corte Inglés. Equally popular among locals are the small eclectic music shops along Carrer Tallers (see p82). Also worth a look are the CD and vinyl music shops on nearby Carrer Riera Baixa (see p82). ✆ FNAC: El Triangle, Pl de Catalunya 4 ✆ El Corte Inglés: Portal de l'Àngel 19–21

9 Late-night Shops

There are numerous late-night grocery stores selling the basics. Open Cor sells everything from fresh flowers to wrapping paper, beer and wine. ✆ Open Cor: Gran Via 407 and Gran de Gràcia 29 • Open until 2am daily

10 Department Stores

Barcelona's leading department store is El Corte Inglés, which has branches across the city. You can find seemingly everything under one roof, including a supermarket and a gourmet food shop. ✆ El Corte Inglés: several locations, including Pl de Catalunya 14, Av Diagonal 471–473 & 617–619

⏵ For Barcelona's best shopping areas **See pp50–51**

Left **Shop sale sign** Centre **Five-euro note** Right **Menú del Dia**

🔟 Barcelona on a Budget

1 Sightseeing Passes

The Barcelona Card offers up to 50 per cent off the city's main attractions, plus free travel on buses and the metro, and free entrance to some of the main museums. It's available for two to five days at all tourist offices and El Corte Inglés department stores. The Articket (€30, valid for six months) provides free entry to six art museums, including MACBA *(see pp28–9)*, the Fundació Joan Miró *(see pp22–3)* and the Museu Picasso *(see pp24–5)*. The tourist office on Plaça de Catalunya *(see p134)* sells it, as do the museums.

2 Museums

Many museums offer free entry on the first Sunday of the month, including the Museu Picasso *(see pp24–5)* and MNAC *(see pp18–19)*. Others are also free 3–8pm every Sunday. The tourist office has a list of all the free museum days. Most museums also offer a 30–50 per cent discount – or free entry – for people over 65.

3 Public Transport

The T-10 ticket permits 10 rides on metro, FGC and buses, and allows for transfers (within 75 minutes). Alternatively, you can purchase a two-, three-, four- or five-day pass, which provides unlimited travel on the same services. See p131.

4 Concerts & Opera

Enjoy rock-bottom prices for concerts and the opera (Sep–Jul) by buying seats with partial views – or no view at all. The Gran Teatre del Liceu *(see p66)* sells cheap tickets for opera and classical recitals. The Palau de la Música Catalana *(see pp26–7)* has reduced price early-evening weekend shows twice a month. A ticket booth at Rambla 99, in front of the Palau de la Virreina *(see p13)*, sells last-minute tickets at discount prices. Ⓢ *Gran Teatre del Liceu ticket office: 93 485 99 00*

5 Eating

The most economical way to get a bite to eat is to pick up picnic goodies at one of the city's food markets *(see pp52–3)*. The *menú del dia* (fixed lunch menu) offered from Monday to Friday at many restaurants is often very reasonable. Dining on the terrace can be more pricey than eating inside, where sitting at the bar is usually the cheapest option.

6 Fast Food

Bypass McDonald's and Burger King and sample Spain's cheaper fast food equivalents. Pans & Company and Bocatta are found all over town; both offer cheap meals, particularly if you eat between 10am and noon, and 4 and 7pm.

7 Drinking

Start out the night in your hotel with a bottle of Spanish wine from the supermarket. Then head to the Barri Gòtic or El Raval where there are plenty of cheap dive bars. Order a *canya* (draught beer) or a Spanish bottled beer, Estrella or Moritz, which are usually cheaper than imported beers.

8 Hotels

Visit Barcelona during the low season, from October to April, and you'll find cheaper hotel deals (and air fares). The same can be true in August when many Spanish businesses close. Enquire about any special deals when booking a room.

9 Hotel Bars

You don't have to stay at the ritzy hotels to enjoy their luxurious environs. Most of the bars and cafés at the five-star hotels are open to the public. Try the Hotel Arts *(see p143)*, or the Hotel W, with its great views *(see p143)*, where you can sip a cocktail to the sound of classical piano.

10 Cinemas

Go to the cinema *(see p67)* on *el dia del espectador* (often Monday or Wednesday) or for a matinée (usually before 2:30pm), when tickets are cheaper.

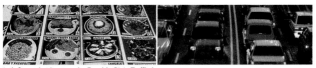

Left **Overpriced eatery, La Rambla** Right **Traffic jam**

Things to Avoid

1 Dangerous Areas

Beware of under-populated alleys and streets in the old town after dark, particularly in the Barri Gòtic and El Raval. These attract thieves who tend to operate in groups. Prime pickpocketing times are between 9pm and midnight, when most locals are eating dinner and only visitors are out on the streets. The early hours (3–6am), after the bars and clubs close, are also popular with thieves.

2 Overpriced Leather Shops

Avoid the pricey leather shops clustered on and around La Rambla. The leather is often poor quality and prices are high. Stop off at the tourist office for a list of approved leather shops, or head for established stores *(see pp50–51).*

3 La Rambla Scams

Don't get sidetracked by the raucous "find the hidden ball" games on La Rambla. Usually played on makeshift tables, presided over by a skilled, nimble-fingered trickster, it appears at first glance to be a lively game of chance. In reality, it's a confidence trick. The lively folk who cheer you on are all accomplices who are in on the act. Though you may win the first few rounds, you'll soon start to lose, and you'll walk away with a much lighter

wallet. Also to be avoided are the gypsies who try to sell you flowers and often pick your pocket at the same time!

4 Overpriced Eats

Rip-off, touristy terrace restaurants line La Rambla. Most of these paella and tapas eateries cater solely to tourists, charging sky-high prices for mediocre meals. The side streets off La Rambla offer better food at more reasonable prices.

5 Crowds

Miss the crowds and interminably long queues at the city's most popular sights by visiting first thing in the morning when the sights open or towards the end of the day, an hour or two before closing time. To avoid the hordes on the beaches in summer go on weekday afternoons.

6 Money Exchange

Steer clear of the bureaux de change on La Rambla, Plaça de Catalunya and near major tourist sights. They usually charge much higher commission than banks. If they advertise no commission, exchange rates are generally poor.

7 Looking Like a Tourist

Avoid attracting attention to yourself as a tourist. Keep cameras hidden, try not to display large banknotes and don't wear

valuable jewellery. When consulting a guidebook or map, keep a vigilant eye on your belongings.

8 Traffic

Avoid city traffic congestion by driving around late morning (10am–1pm) or late afternoon (5–7pm). Most office workers have a lunch break between 2pm and 4pm, which means that the roads are packed during this period. Similarly, avoid leaving town on Friday evenings, particularly during the summer. The best time to head out of the city is mid- to late-morning after 10am.

9 August

During the month of August, many Barcelona establishments shut down altogether, the locals disappear on holiday and the city fills with visitors. With so many restaurants, bars, shops and even some sights closed, not to mention the distinct lack of local life, August in Barcelona has its drawbacks. Always call first to check on opening times during this period.

10 Monday Sightseeing

Many of the top museums are closed on Mondays, including the Museu Picasso *(see pp24–5)* and the MNAC *(see pp18–19).* So always double-check opening times on this day.

Left **Room, Hotel Mesón Castilla** Right **Suite, Hotel Claris**

TOP 10 Accommodation Tips

1 Book Ahead
If visiting Barcelona in the high season (Mar–Jul & Sep), book ahead as the city's hotels, *pensions* and *hostals* (smaller, more basic guesthouses) usually fill to capacity. Ask about special deals, especially in the low season. Booking through the hotel's website is usually the cheapest option. Note that a tourist tax (€1–2.50 per night per person aged 16 and over) is charged for a maximum of seven nights.

2 Where to Find Budget Beds
There are scores of cheap *pensions* and *hostals* on La Rambla and its sidestreets in the Barri Gòtic and El Raval. Plaça Reial also has a cluster of budget accommodation options.

3 Pensions & Hostals
Room size (and comfort level) in *pensions* and *hostals* varies widely, but in the accredited budget places (the tourist office has a list of these), you'll find clean rooms and good security. Rooms come either *amb bany* (with a bath) or *sense bany* (without a bath); most have a washbasin.

4 Getting the Room you Want
Hotels and *hostals* give the best rooms to those who ask for them – so always inquire. Most

hostals, particularly in the old town, have some rooms with wrought-iron balconies, which can make all the difference to a small room. Ask for *una habitació exterior amb vistes* (a room with a view) or *amb balcó* (with balcony). If you're a light sleeper, opt for *una habitació interior* (interior room).

5 Single Travellers
Single rooms at *hostals* and *pensions* are few and far between, but hotels are legally obliged to let double rooms to single occupants at a fixed price. All rates must be posted at reception or in the rooms.

6 Families
Many hotels offer discounts for children under 12 when they share their parents' room on a temporary bed.

7 Security
If you're going to be staying at youth hostels and campsites, carry a chain and padlock to tie your luggage to something sturdy. Always leave your valuables in a safe or locked box, which most places have.

8 Hotel Booking Service & Websites
The tourist office *(see p132)* in Plaça de Catalunya has a hotel booking service, which is useful if you arrive in high season without a

reservation. It offers bookings in hotels of all categories, but most often in three-star hotels and above. A deposit is payable on reservation. The tourist office also produces a list of the best *pensions* and *hostals* for budget travellers. On the web, try www.budget places.com and www. barcelonaturisme.com.

9 Cases de Pagès
Discover rural Catalonia by staying at *Cases de Pagès* (country or farm houses), which offer B&B-style lodgings. They vary widely, from small, rural homes with a handful of rooms to luxurious, palace-sized farmhouses. Stop by the Turisme de Catalunya office *(see p132)* for a free list of the *Gîtes de Catalunya* and (to buy) the *Cases de Pagès* book, which has detailed listings. This information is also on the website (www.gencat.cat/probert).

10 Refugis
Throughout the Pyrenees and other mountainous areas, you'll find *refugis* (basic mountain hostels). They offer simple, cheap accommodation, usually bunk beds in a dorm room. In the summer months, *refugis* fill up quickly, so it is advisable to book in advance. Ask at tourist offices for a list of local ones; or stop by Turisme de Catalunya *(see p132).*

 Visitors seeking long-term accommodation, beware of agencies that charge for accommodation lists; they are invariably a scam.

Price Categories

For a standard, double room per night (with breakfast if included), taxes and extra charges.

€	Under €60
€€	€60–120
€€€	€120–180
€€€€	€180–240
€€€€€	Over €240

Hotel Omm

🔟 Luxury Hotels

1 Hotel Arts
Barcelona's grande dame five-star hotel is mere steps from the sea, with ample, sumptuous rooms and top-notch eating places. The first-floor, outdoor pool has stunning views. ✪ *C/Marina 19–21 • Map G5 • 93 221 10 00 • www.hotelartsbarcelona. com • DA • €€€€€*

2 Abac Hotel and Restaurant
Arguably the city's finest restaurant, Abac is part of a boutique hotel with 15 gorgeous rooms stylishly decorated with contemporary minimalism. There is a spa and a small, but immaculate, garden. ✪ *Avda Tibidabo 1 • 93 319 66 00 • www.abac barcelona.com • DA • €€€€€*

3 Hotel Palace Barcelona
This deluxe hotel, is an emblem of tradition and style, with great service. The famous Restaurant Caelis offers an innovative gourmet menu. ✪ *Gran Via de les Corts Catalanes, 668 • Map F3 • 93 510 11 30 • www. hotelpalacebarcelona.com • DA • €€€€€*

4 Hotel Majestic
Stately decor and faultless service are the hallmarks of this aptly named hotel. Exit through the heavy brass-and-glass doors and you're mere steps from the Eixample's *Modernista* gems. The

rooftop plunge pool has views of the Sagrada Família and the Barcelona cityscape. ✪ *Pg de Gràcia 68 • Map E2 • 93 492 22 44 • www.hotelmajestic.es • DA • €€€€€*

5 Hotel Omm
Designed by award-winning Catalan architect Juli Capella, this is one of the hottest hotels in the city. There is an excellent restaurant and bar *(see p107)*, a great spa and stunning views from the rooftop deck and pool. ✪ *C/Rosselló 265 • Map E2 • 93 445 40 00 • www. hotelomm.es • DA • €€€€€*

6 Hotel W
Popularly known as the Hotel Vela (the sail hotel) for its billowing form, this sumptuous five-star option enjoys unparalleled sea views. With floor-to-ceiling windows it is easy to imagine you are at sea. All the fancy extras are here, from spa and rooftop pool to designer bars and restaurants. ✪ *Plaça de la Rosa dels Vents 1 • Map E5 • 93 295 28 00 • www.w-barcelona.com • DA • €€€€€*

7 Granados 83
Rooms at this designer hotel are decorated with African zebrawood, chocolate brown leather and original pieces of Buddhist and Hindu art. Suites have private terraces overlooking a plunge pool. There is a restaurant, and a pretty

rooftop pool with a very fashionable bar. ✪ *C/Enric Granados 83 • Map E2 • 93 492 96 70 • www.derbyhotels.com • DA • €€€€*

8 Casa Camper
A converted 19th-century mansion, this hotel oozes with innovative yet comfortable design touches. Big rooms, roof-terrace, extraordinary vertical garden and a free 24-hour bar. ✪ *C/Elisabets 11 • Map L2 • 93 342 62 80 • www.casacamper.com • DA • €€€€*

9 Hotel Rey Juan Carlos I
This massive complex includes a vast private garden and a conference hall for up to 2,500 people. The spacious rooms are sumptuously decorated in a contemporary style. The top floors offer unobstructed views of the city and mountains. ✪ *Av Diagonal 661–671 • Off map • 93 364 40 40 • www.hrjuan carlos.com • DA • €€€*

10 Grand Hotel Central
This large, elegant hotel has a great location close to the Gothic Quarter and Born. But the real draw is the stunning rooftop infinity pool with spectacular views of the city. ✪ *Via Laietana 30 • Map E4 • 93 295 79 00 • www.grandhotelcentral. com • €€€€*

Left **Salon, Hotel Mesón Castilla** Right **Hotel 1898**

TOP 10 Historical Hotels

1 Hotel Mesón Castilla

A historical gem in the heart of El Raval, this family-run hotel is housed in an early-1900s mansion. A home-turned-hotel, it shines under the loving care of its management. From the opulent first-floor salon to the lovely rooms – each with antique furniture – this hotel offers a chance to step back in time. 🕲 *C/Valldonzella 5 • Map L1 • 93 318 21 82 • www. mesoncastilla.com • €€€*

2 Hotel España

Housed in a building dating back to 1859, which was renovated by the Modernist architect Lluís Domènich i Montaner, this luxurious hotel has a roof terrace with swimming pool. 🕲 *Sant Pau 9 • Map L4 • 93 550 00 00 • www.hotel espanya.com • DA • €€€*

3 Gran Hotel La Florida

Set in a Modernista villa in the hills above Barcelona, this luxurious hotel has been beautifully renovated by the finest designers and architects. 🕲 *Ctra Vallvidrera al Tibidabo 83-93 • 93 259 30 00 • www.hotellaflorida.com • DA • €€€€*

4 Hotel Neri

This 17th-century former palace at the heart of the Barri Gòtic offers an exclusive combination of history, the avant-garde

and glamour. There is Internet access in all rooms, a library, solarium and a roof terrace with views to the Cathedral. 🕲 *C/Sant Sever 5 • Map M3 • 93 304 06 55 • www. hotelneri.com • €€€€€*

5 Hotel Mercer

This boutique hotel in the Old Town offers 28 large and comfortable rooms. Although some features, such as the beamed ceilings, are original, the decor has a cutting-edge, designer feel to it. There are amazing views of the city from the swimming pool on the roof terrace, and a restaurant and cocktail bar. 🕲 *Carrer Lledó 7 • Map N4 • 93 310 74 80 • www.mercerbarcelona. com • DA • €€€€€*

6 1898

A 19th-century tobacco factory houses this chic hotel, which has retained some original fittings and combined them with 21st-century amenities. These include pools, a fitness centre and spa, and a good restaurant. 🕲 *La Rambla 109 • Map L2 • 93 552 95 52 • www.hotel1898.com • DA • €€€€*

7 Hotel Duquesa de Cardona

Located in a 16th-century building, this stylish hotel combines the original structure with avant-garde decor and all the modern facilities. The rooftop

terrace, which offers great views over the Port Vell, also has a plunge pool. 🕲 *Passeig Colón 12 • Map M6 • 93 268 90 90 • www.hduquesade cardona.com • DA • €€€€*

8 Hotel Montecarlo

This friendly, family-owned hotel, with a 1930s façade, is particularly eye-catching lit up at night. Rooms are pleasant and bright, and many have balconies overlooking La Rambla. 🕲 *Ramblas 124 • Map L2 • 93 412 04 04 • www.montecarlobcn. com • €€*

9 Casa Fuster

Originally designed by Domènech i Muntaner, this hotel is one of the city's most prestigious and luxurious. The sumptuous *Modernista* details have been retained, but are combined with 21st-century amenities. 🕲 *Passeig de Gràcia 132 • Map E1 • 93 255 30 00 • www.hotelescenter.es/ casafuster • DA • €€€€€*

10 Hotel Claris

This 19th-century Eixample palace was once home to the counts of Vedruna. Inside is a small museum of pre-Colombian art, some of which also decorates the suites. Guests get free admission to the Museu Egipci *(see p105)*, run by the hotel owner. 🕲 *C/Pau Claris 150 • Map E2 • 93 487 62 62 • www.derby hotels.com • DA • €€€€*

It is always worth checking hotel websites for off-season promotional offers.

Price Categories

For a standard, double room per night (with breakfast if included), taxes and extra charges.

€	under €60
€€	€60–120
€€€	€120–180
€€€€	€180–240
€€€€€	over €240

Exterior, Hotel Colón

Streetsmart

🔟 Central Stays

1 Hotel Colón
A handsome, family-owned Barri Gòtic hotel, the Colón has traditional decor with mirrors and oil paintings throughout. The magnificent views of the Cathedral and Plaça de la Seu from this homely, quaint place, are stunning. Ⓢ Av de la Catedral 7 • Map N3 • 93 301 14 04 • www.colonhotel barcelona.com • €€€

2 Room Mate Emma
A great option if you're looking for style on a budget, the Room Mate Emma offers compact but gorgeously designed bedrooms in the very centre of the city. There's no restaurant, but the staff will happily give recommendations. Ⓢ C/Rosselló 205 • Map E2 • 93 238 56 06 • www.room-matehotels. com • €€

3 Hotel Chic & Basic
This converted 19th-century townhouse is a big hit with fashionistas. Rooms are minimalist with contemporary glass and steel bathrooms, and colourful LED lights that add a kitsch touch. The White Bar is very popular, as is the restaurant, Kharma. There's a common area where you can chat to other guests. Ⓢ C/ Princesa 50 • Map P4 • 93 295 46 52 • www. chicandbasic.com • €€€

4 Hotel Banys Orientals
Behind the traditional frontage lies a modern, cosy hotel with free Internet access in every room. Plusher suites are available in a separate building. The Cathedral, Picasso museum and Barceloneta beach are close by. Ⓢ C/Argenteria 37 • Map N4 • 93 268 84 60 • www.hotelbanys orientals.com • €€

5 Mandarin Oriental Barcelona
This ultra-luxurious hotel boasts rooms overlooking either the iconic Passeig de Gràcia or the gorgeous interior gardens. It has a spa, a roof terrace with splash pool and gourmet restaurant, Moments. Ⓢ Passeig de Gràcia 38–40 • Map E3 • 93 151 88 88 • www.mandarinoriental. com/barcelona • DA • €€€€€

6 Park Hotel
A 1950s design classic with a gorgeous wrap-around staircase, the Park Hotel was refurbished by the original architect's son. Rooms are small but comfortably furnished, and some have balconies. It is near the fashionable Born boutiques and clubs. Ⓢ Avinguda Marquès de l'Argentera 11 • Map F5 • 93 319 60 00 • www.park hotelbarcelona.com • €€€

7 Jazz
The modern Jazz hotel may not be the most characterful option, but it is centrally located and has many amenities including a small rooftop pool. It is great value for money, and the friendly staff are always on-hand to offer help and advice. Ⓢ C/Pelai 3 • Map L1 • 93 552 96 96 • www. hoteljazz.com • DA • €€€

8 Hotel Constanza
This elegant mid-sized hotel is located near all the main sights of Eixample. Some of the stylish rooms come with terraces and there is a good guest-only restaurant. Ⓢ C/Bruc 33 • Map F3 • 93 270 19 10 • www.hotelconstanza. com • DA • €€€

9 Soho
Top Spanish architect Alfredo Arribas, designed this swanky hotel. Located in Eixample, it's perfect for shopping, sightseeing and enjoying the nightlife. Ⓢ Gran Vía Corts Catalanes 543 • Map D3 • 93 552 96 10 • www.hotelsohobarcelona. com • DA • €€€

10 Pullman Barcelona
Located on the beach-front, the Pullman has the perfect location for a summer city-break. It has all the facilities you would expect in a five-star hotel. Designed for business travellers, weekend bargains are often available. Ⓢ Avenida Litoral 10 • Map G6 • 93 221 65 65 • www.pullman-barcelona-skipper.com • DA • €€€€

Unless otherwise stated, all hotels accept credit cards, have en-suite bathrooms and air conditioning.

Left **Hostal Jardí** Right **Entrance hall, Hostal Oliva**

Budget Accommodation

Sol y k
A charming budget option in the heart of the Gothic quarter. A handful of individually decorated rooms with mosaic head-boards and original artworks set the Sol y k apart from other guest houses in this price bracket. Some rooms are en-suite. Free Wi-Fi is available. ✆ *C/Cervantes 2 • Map M5 • 93 318 81 48 • www.solyk.com • €*

Hostal Oliva
From the lovely, *Modernista* elevator to the individually wrapped soaps, this cheerful, family-run *hostal* is one of Barcelona's best. The ornate *Modernista* build-ing has bright rooms that are sparklingly clean; some have en-suite bath-rooms. ✆ *Pg de Gràcia 32 • Map E3 • 93 488 01 62 • www.hostaloliva.com • No credit cards • €€*

Hostal Goya
A well-run *hostal* established in 1952. The rooms are bright and modern, with bold prints and some designer touches. Most rooms have en-suite bathrooms and some have air conditioning. Apartments are also available. ✆ *C/ Pau Claris 74 • Map N1 • 93 302 25 65 • www. hostalgoya.com • €€*

Praktik
This centrally located budget hotel is set in a sumptuous *Modernista* mansion. The original turn-of-the-20th-century tiling and carved woodwork make a striking contrast with the contemporary furnishings. There are only a handful of rooms, so book early. ✆ *Rambla de Catalunya 27 • Map E3 • 93 343 66 90 • www.hotel praktikrambla.com • €€*

Market
Close to the *Modernista* market of Sant Antoni, this is a very stylish hotel for the price. The rooms have an oriental feel, with glossy lacquered wood and a red-white-and-black colour theme. Breakfast is served in the popular restaurant. Book well in advance. ✆ *Comte Borrell 68 • Map D3 • 93 325 12 05 • www.markethotel. com.es • €€*

Hostal Jardí
Get your beauty sleep in the snug heart of the Barri Gòtic at this hostel. Simple yet spotless rooms, all with en-suite bathrooms, are done up in light wood and cool colours. The bright breakfast room has balconies overlooking the plaça. ✆ *Pl Sant Josep Oriol 1 • Map M3 • 93 301 59 00 • www.eljardi-barcelona.com • €€*

El Balcon del Born
This charming guest-house in the fashionable Born district has just three delightful rooms (with private or shared bathrooms). Each is individually decorated and with its own balcony. Book early. ✆ *C/Rera Palau 2 • Map P5 • 63 452 45 05 (mobile) • €€*

Bonic
A great budget option, this charming hotel has stylish rooms and many thoughtful extras, such as free tea, coffee, muffins, Internet access and dressing gowns. Bathrooms, however, are shared. ✆ *C/Josep Anselm Clavé 9 • Map L6 • 62 605 34 34 (mobile) • www.bonic-barcelona.com • €€*

Hotel Acta Mimic
Close to Las Ramblas, this hotel is in a building that used to house a theatre. Rooms are bright and airy, with large windows and sleek, modern decor. Guests can relax on the hammocks on the roof terrace, which doubles as a solarium with a view over the Old Town and the port. ✆ *C/Arc del Teatre 58 • Map K5 • 93 329 94 50 • www.hotel-mimic.com • DA • €€€*

Hotel Chic and Basic Zoo
In the heart of the Born district is this unusual hotel offering rooms described as Single, M, L and XL. XL rooms have balconies facing Ciutadella Park. ✆ *Passeig Picasso 22 • Map Q4 • 93 315 08 60 • www. chicandbasic.com • €€*

Unless otherwise stated, none of these establishments has air conditioning or en-suite bathrooms.

Price Categories

For a standard, double room per night (with breakfast if included), taxes and extra charges.

€ under €60
€€ €60–120
€€€ €120–180
€€€€ €180–240
€€€€€ over €240

First floor, Equity Point Youth Hostel

Hostels and Student Residences

Equity Point Youth Hostel

This bright, well-run, central hostel has dorm rooms sleeping 6 to 14. Breakfast is included in the price, and there's free 24-hour Internet access. There is air conditioning in all rooms. ❧ C/Vigatans 5 • Map N4 • 93 268 78 08 • www.equity-point.com • €

Sant Jordi Aragó Hostel

This award-winning hostel is ideally located next to the Passeig de Gràcia. There are dorm rooms for four to 10 guests, a lounge area with DVD player, computers with free 24-hour Internet access, and a fully equipped kitchen. ❧ C/Aragó 268 • Map E2 • 93 215 67 43 • www.sant jordihostels.com • €

Feetup Hostel-Garden House

This friendly hostel is located on the outskirts of the city, near the beautiful Gaudí-designed Park Güell. It's only a 15-minute metro ride into the centre of town. There is a lovely garden and roof terrace, and a relaxed vibe. ❧ C/ d'Hedilla 58 • 93 427 24 79 • www. feetuphostels.com • €

Hostal V Downtown

Established by four former travellers, this friendly hostel is a hit with young backpackers. It is central, has no curfew, you don't need to rent sheets and blankets, and it offers a range of rooms, with or without bathrooms. ❧ C/Junta de Comerç 13 • Map K4 • 93 302 61 34 • www. hostaldowntownbarcelona. com • €€

Alberg Kabul

Kabul is a favourite with young backpackers, so it's often full (and noisy). Dorm rooms, all with air conditioning and some with balconies on the Plaça Reial (see p36), sleep 4 to 20 people. There's a laundry, free Internet access, lockers and a small cafeteria that serves cheap food during the day. ❧ Pl Reial 17 • Map L4 • 93 318 51 90 • www.kabul.es • €

Barcelona Dream

This hostel is a 20-minute metro ride from the city centre, but close to the beaches. It is well-priced, and the rooms accommodate between two and 12 guests. Kitchen and laundry facilities are included. ❧ Ave. Alfonso XIII 28b, Badalona • 93 399 14 20 • www.barcelonadream.net • €

Equity Point Centric Hostel

Housed in a renovated Modernista building, this hostel offers large dorms, as well as single and double rooms with private facilities. There is a common room with a bar, free Internet access and satellite TV. ❧ Passeig de Gràcia 33 • Map E3 • 93 231 20 45 • www. equity-point.com • €

Melon District

Part-student residence and part-hostel, Melon District has rooms available to rent for short- or long-term stays. The rooms are not large, but have great facilities. There is a rooftop plunge pool. ❧ Avda Paral.lel 101 • Map D4 • 93 217 88 12 • www. melondistrict.com • €€

Mambo Tango

Toto and Marino, ex-travellers themselves, are behind this warm and welcoming hostel. It has dorms for four, six and eight people, breakfast and sheet-hire are included in the price, and extras include a home cinema. Party animals are actively discouraged, so you can count on a good night's sleep. ❧ C/Poeta Cabanyes 23 • Map C4 • 93 442 51 64 • www. hostelmambotango.com • €

Itaca Hostel

In the heart of the Gothic Quarter, this is a clean and friendly hostel with space for 30 guests in double rooms, dorms (for up to six) and apartments. Bedding and lockers are included in the price and there is Wi-Fi available in the main building. ❧ C/Ripoll 21 • Map N3 • 93 301 97 51 • www.itacahostel.com • €

Left **Camping Tamariu** Right **Swimming Pool, Aparthotel Bertran**

TOP10 Campsites and Aparthotels

1 Camping Roca-Grossa

Situated between the mountains and the sea, this modern campsite has good installations and access to the nearby beach. It has a large swimming pool, restaurant and bar and is 1 km from the lively resort of Calella. Bungalows are also available. ◉ *Ctra, N-II km 665, Calella • 93 769 12 97 • www.rocagrossa.com • Closed Oct–Mar • €*

2 Camping Sitges

A small and well-kept campsite with swimming pool, supermarket and playground. It is located 2 kms (1 mile) southward from Sitges, and is close to its famous beaches. ◉ *Ctra Comarcal C-246a, km 38, Sitges • 93 894 10 80 • www.camping sitges.com • Closed mid-Oct–Feb • €*

3 Camping Masnou Barcelona

Located 12 km (7.5 miles) to the north of Barcelona, this family-owned campsite faces the sea and has a small beach nearby. Facilities include a supermarket, swimming pool and bar. ◉ *Camilo Fabra 33 (N-II, km 663), El Masnou • 93 555 15 03 • www.campingmasnou barcelona.com • Credit cards from €100 • DA • €*

4 Camping Tamariu

This well-kept camp site is on the Costa Brava, near the lovely beach town of Tamariu. It is 200 m (656 ft) from the beach and within sauntering distance of the town for bars, restaurants and grocery shops. ◉ *Costa Rica 2, near Tamariu, 5 km E of Palafrugell • 97 262 04 22 • www.campingtamariu. com • Closed Oct–Apr • €*

5 Camping Barcelona

Located 28km (17.5 miles) north of Barcelona is this campsite next to a small beach. It is also close to several larger beaches. The camp site is about 1 km (0.6 mile) from the train station. Bungalows are also available. ◉ *Carretera N-II, km 650, 8 km E of Mataró • 93 790 47 20 • www. campingbarcelona.com • Closed Nov–Mar • DA • €*

6 Camping Globo Rojo

Close to the beaches of Canet de Mar and with a swimming pool, tennis court, football pitch as well as all kinds of sporting activities. Great for kids. Direct bus service to Barcelona. ◉ *Ctra N-II km 660, 9, Canet de Mar • 93 794 11 43 • www. globo-rojo.com • Closed Oct–Mar • DA • €*

7 Citadines

If you're smitten with Barcelona, try an aparthotel for a longer stay. The Citadines aparthotel on La Rambla has well-appointed studios and small apartments with amenities, such as a kitchen (with oven and microwave), iron and a CD stereo. The rooftop solarium, equipped with beach chairs and showers, is just the spot to unwind. ◉ *La Rambla 122 • Map L2 • 93 270 11 11 • www. citadines.com • €€€*

8 Aparthotel Bertran

This aparthotel has ample studios and apartments (many with balconies), a rooftop terrace with swimming pool, a small gym and 24-hour laundry service. Breakfast is served in your apartment. ◉ *C/Bertran 150 • 93 212 75 50 • www.bertran-hotel.com • €€*

9 Atenea Aparthotel

Designed with business travellers in mind, this top-notch aparthotel sits near Barcelona's business and financial district around upper Diagonal. Rooms are ample and well-equipped, and there are several conference rooms and a 24-hour laundry service. ◉ *C/Joan Güell 207–211 • 93 490 66 40 • www.cityhotels.es • €€*

10 Oh Barcelona

This company has a huge number of apartments in and around the city. Prices for a one-bedroom apartment range from €55 to €140 per night. ◉ *93 467 37 79 • www.oh-barcelona.com*

Unless otherwise stated, all campsites are open all year round, though many open only at weekends October–March.

Price Categories

For a standard, double room per night (with breakfast if included), taxes and extra charges.

€ under €60
€€ €60–120
€€€ €120–180
€€€€ €180–240
€€€€€ over €240

Coastline, Costa Brava

Getaways Beyond Barcelona

El Castell de la Ciutat

Located next to a 16th-century castle, this offers refined luxury in the heart of the Pyrenees. There are a couple of restaurants, a spa, beautiful gardens, indoor and outdoor pools, and wonderful mountain views. ◈ *Crta. N-260, km 229, La Seu d'Urgell • 97 335 00 00 • www.hotel-castell-ciutat.com • €€€€€*

Aiguaclara

This charming hotel-restaurant is located in a whitewashed 19th-century villa in the centre of Begur. The beautiful rooms are a mix of contemporary furnishings and original features. The wonderful restaurant and outstanding service make this the ideal place for a romantic break. ◈ *C/Sant Miquel 2, Begur • 97 262 29 05 • www.hotelaigua clara.com • €€€*

Hotel Aiguablava

This coastal institution is perched atop rugged cliffs overlooking the Mediterranean. It is run by the fourth generation of the same family. Many of the rooms – each individually decorated – have splendid vistas of the sea. There's a large outdoor pool and breakfast is included. Apartments are also available. ◈ *Platja de Fornells, Begur • 97 262 20 58 • www.hotelaigua blava.com • Closed mid-Oct–late Mar • €€€*

Fonda Biayna

The Fonda Biayna has been in operation since the 1820s. Wood-beamed ceilings and antique furniture imbue it with rustic flair. The inn's most famous guest was Picasso, who arrived here by mule en route to Paris (with paintings in tow). ◈ *C/de Sant Roc 11, Bellver de Cerdanya • 97 351 04 75 • www. fondabiayna.com • €€*

Hostal Sa Tuna

Take in the sea views from your terrace at this five-room, family-run hotel on the pretty Platja Sa Tuna. The restaurant serves excellent Catalan cuisine and breakfast is included. ◈ *Pg de Ancora 6, Platja Sa Tuna, 5 km N of Begur • 97 262 21 98 • www.hostalsatuna.com • Closed Oct–Mar • €€€*

Blau Mar

A delightful hotel in a charming seaside village, Blau Mar has traditionally decorated rooms (most with terraces), lovely gardens and a pool with amazing views out to sea. There are superb clifftop walks and stunning coves in the vicinity. ◈ *C/Farena 36, Llafranc • 97 261 00 55 • http://hotelblaumar llafranc.com • €€€€*

Parador de Tortosa

Looming over the town of Tortosa is the ancient Arab Castillo de la Zuda, within which this parador is housed. Decor is suitably old-world, with dark-wood furniture and antique fixtures, and the view of countryside and mountains is superb. ◈ *Castillo de la Zuda, Tortosa • 97 744 44 50 • www.parador.es • €€€*

Ca L'Aliu

This restored, cosy *casa rural* is in the tiny medieval town of Pera-tallada. Comfortable rooms all have antique furniture. The amiable owners will lend you bikes. ◈ *C/Roca 6, Peratallada, 12 km NW of Palafrugell • 97 263 40 61 • www. calaliu.com • €€*

Val de Neu

Perhaps the most sumptuous ski hotel in the chic resort of Baqueria Beret, Val de Neu is located right next to the slopes. Among the five-star amenities are a spa, a pool and an array of restaurants. ◈ *C/Perimetrau s/n • 97 363 50 00 • www.hotel baqueiravaldeneu.com • Closed May–Sep • €€€€€*

Hotel Historic

A good base for visiting Girona, this hotel is located in the heart of the old quarter. Choose from rooms or self-catering apartments, just around the corner from the cathedral. ◈ *C/Belmirall 4a, Girona • 97 222 35 83 • www. hotelhistoric.com • €€€*

General Index

Acknowledgements

The Authors
Travel writer, reporter and editor AnneLise Sorensen is half-Catalan and has lived and worked in Barcelona. She has penned (and wine tasted) her way across four continents, contributing to guidebooks, magazines, newspapers, TV and radio.

Ryan Chandler is a writer and journalist who has been working in Barcelona for over ten years. He currently works as Barcelona correspondent for the Spanish magazine *The Broadsheet*.

Produced by Departure Lounge, London

Editorial Director Ella Milroy
Art Editor Lee Redmond
Editor Clare Tomlinson
Designer Lisa Kosky
DTP Designer Ingrid Vienings
Picture Researcher Monica Allende
Research Assistance Amaia Allende, Ana Virginia Aranha, Diveen Henry
Consultant Brian Catlos
Proofreader Catherine Day
Indexer Hilary Bird
Fact Checkers Paula Canal, Brian Catlos, Mary-Ann Gallagher, AnneLise Sorensen

Photographers Joan Farré, Manuel Huguet

Additional photography Ian Aitken, Max Alexander, Mike Dunning, Steve Gorton, Heidi Grassley, Alan Keohane, Rita Merino, Rough Guides/Chris Christoforou, Ella Milroy, Naomi Peck, Aureila Caro Sanchez, Paul Young
Illustrators Chris Orr & Associates, Lee Redmond
Maps Martin Darlison, Tom Coulson,

Encompass Graphics Ltd

AT DORLING KINDERSLEY
Senior Publishing Manager Louise Bostock Lang
Publishing Manager Kate Poole
Senior Art Editor Marisa Renzullo
Art Director Gillian Allan
Publisher Douglas Amrine
Cartography Co-ordinator Casper Morris
DTP Jason Little, Conrad van Dyk
Production Joanna Bull
Revisions Team
Namrata Adhwaryu, Emma Anacootee, Claire Baranowski, Marta Bescos, Sonal Bhatt, Mariana Evmolpidou, Anna Freiberger, Mary-Ann Gallagher, Lydia Halliday, Integrated Publishing Solutions, Claire Jones, Bharti Karakoti, Juliet Kenny, Jude Ledger, Nicola Malone, Alison McGill, Caroline Mead, Vikki Nousiainen, Pete Quinlan, Quadrum Solutions, Mani Ramaswamy, Julie Thompson, Sands Publishing Solutions, Hugo Wilkinson, Word On Spain

Picture Credits
Key: a-above; b-below/bottom; c-centre; f-far; l-left; r-right; t-top.

Works of art have been reproduced with permission of the following copyright holders: *Homea* 1974 Eduardo Arranz Bravo © ADAGP, Paris and DACS, London 2011 28br; *Rainy Taxi* Salvador Dalí © Kingdom of Spain, Gala–Salvador Dalí Foundation, DACS, London 2011 119b.

The publishers would like to thank the following individuals, companies and picture libraries for permission to reproduce their photographs:
AGUA RESTAURANT: 101tl; AISA, Barcelona: 1c, 11c, 30tl, 30tr, 30c, 31bl, 31tr, 31cr, 31br, 118c; ALAMY

MAGES: ICSDB 131tr; Melvyn Longhurst 61bl; BASÍLICA DE LA SAGRADA FAMILIA: Pep Daudé 9ca; BARCELONA TURISME: 61tr; 110c; 34tr; Espai d'Imatge 64c; 65b; Jordi Trullas 64t; BOBBYGIN: 116tl. CAELUM: 78tr; CA L'ISIDRE: 87tl; CAL PEP: 79t; CASA ALFONSO: 108tr; CASA CALVET: 109tl; CINC SENTITS: 44tl; CLUB CATWALK: 100tl; COMERÇ 24: 44tr. DANIEL CAMPI: 146tl. EGO GALLERY: 84tl; EL PIANO: 114tr; ELEPHANT CLUB: 46ca, 46tc; FUNDACIÓ "LA CAIXA": 8tc, 110tr, 112cl; FUNDACIÓN FRANCISCO GODIA: 104tl; FUNDACIÓN JOAN MIRO: Pagès Catalá al cla de Luna Joan Miró © Sucession Miró/ADAGP, Paris and DACS, London 2011 22bl; Tapis de al Fundacio Joan Miró © Sucession Miró/ADAGP, Paris and DACS, London 2011 22–3c; Home i Dona Davant un Munt d'Excrement Joan Miró © Succession Miró/ADAGP, Paris and DACS, London 2011 23tr; GALERIA DELS ANGELS: 84tl; GETTY IMAGES: Tony Stone/Luc Beziat 48c; GRUPO TRAGALUZ: 42bl, 107tr, 143tl; GUANTERIA Y COMPLEMENTOS ALONSO: 75tr. HOFMANN: 117tl; HOLALA PLAZA: 85tl; MANUEL HUGUET: 128–9. IMAGESTATE: AGE Fotostock 141tr; Courtesy of CAIXA CATALUNYA: 137tl; JAMBOREE:

47tr, 77tr; EL JARDI: 43cla; LA MANUAL ALPARGAT-ERA: 75tc; MON DE MONES: 114tl; MUSEU NACIONAL d'ART DE CATALUNYA: 18b; 19tl; 19tr; 19ca; 19b; 92–93; MUSEU d'ART CONTEMPORANI (MACBA): 28tl; 28cl; 29tl; 28–29c MUSEU PICASSO: Hombre con Boina Pablo Picasso © Sucession Picasso/DACS, London 2011 24b; La Espera Pablo Picasso © Sucession Picasso/DACS, London 2011 24–5; El Loco Pablo Picasso © Sucession Picasso/DACS, London 2011 25t; Sketch for Guernica Pablo Picasso © Sucession Picasso/DACS, London 2011 25cr; Las Meninas Pablo Picasso © Sucession Picasso/DACS, London 2011 25b; MIRIAM NEGRE: 44tr; 46bl; 58bl; 114l; 144r; 112b; 113t; 139r; NÚÑEZ I NAVARRO HOTELS: 144tr; OTTOZUTZ GROUP: 107tl; PARC ZOOLOGIC: 16bl; FRANCISCO FERNANDEZ PRIETO: 76tl; 76tr; PRISMA, Barcelona: 66b; 125t; 126t; RAZZMATAZZ: Albert Uriach 47cl; 100tr; RENFE: 132tr; RESTAURANT IGUELDO: 45clb; SALA BECOOL: 46bl; SIDECAR FACTORY CLUB: Moises Torne (motobi@terra.es) 77tl; THE TATAMI ROOM: 95tl; ZELIG: 86tl; ZENTRAUS: 86tr.

All other images are © Dorling Kindersley. For further information see www.dkimages.com.

Special Editions of DK Travel Guides

DK Travel Guides can be purchased in bulk quantities at discounted prices for use in promotions or as premiums. We are also able to offer special editions and personalized jackets, corporate imprints, and excerpts from all of our books, tailored specifically to meet your own needs.

To find out more, please contact:
(in the United States) **specialsales@dk.com**
(in the UK) **travelspecialsales @uk.dk.com**
(in Canada) DK Special Sales at **general@tourmaline.ca**
(in Australia) **business.development @pearson.com.au**

English-Catalan Phrase Book

In an Emergency

Help!	**Auxili!**	ow-**gzee**-lee
Stop!	**Pareu!**	**pah**-reh-oo
Call a doctor!	**Telefoneu un metge!**	teh-leh-fon-**eh**-oo oon **meh**-djuh
Call an ambulance!	**Telefoneu una ambulància!**	teh-leh-fon-**eh**-oo oo-nah ahm-boo-**lahn**-see-ah
Call the police!	**Telefoneu la policia**	teh-leh-fon-**eh**-oo lah poh-lee-**see**-ah
Call the fire brigade!	**Telefoneu els bombers!**	teh-leh-fon-oo uhlz boom-**behs**
Where is the nearest telephone?	**On és el telèfon més proper?**	on-ehs uhl tuh-leh fon meh-s proo-**peh**
Where is the nearest hospital?	**On és l'hospital més proper?**	on-ehs looss-pee-**tahl** mehs proo-**peh**

Communication Essentials

Yes	**Sí**	see
No	**No**	noh
Please	**Si us plau**	sees **plah**-oo
Thank you	**Gràcies**	**grah**-see-uhs
Excuse me	**Perdoni**	puhr-**thoh**-nee
Hello	**Hola**	**oh**-lah
Goodbye	**Adéu**	ah-they-**oo**
Good night	**Bona nit**	bo-nah **neet**
Morning	**El matí**	uhl muh-**tee**
Afternoon	**La tarda**	lah **tahr**-thuh
Evening	**El vespre**	uhl **vehs**-pruh
Yesterday	**Ahir**	ah-**ee**
Today	**Avui**	uh-voo-ee
Tomorrow	**Demà**	duh-**mah**
Here	**Aquí**	uh-**kee**
There	**Allà**	uh-**lyah**
What?	**Què?**	keh
When?	**Quan?**	kwahn
Why?	**Per què?**	puhr keh
Where?	**On?**	ohn

Useful Phrases

How are you?	**Com està?**	kom uhs-**tah**
Very well, thank you.	**Molt bé, gràcies.**	mol **beh** grah-see-uhs
Pleased to meet you.	**Molt de gust.**	mol duh **goost**
See you soon.	**Fins aviat.**	feenz uhv-**yat**
That's fine.	**Està bé.**	uhs-**tah** beh
Where is/are ..?	**On és/són?**	ohn ehs/sohn
How far is it to ..?	**Quants metres/ kilòmetres hi ha d'aquí a ...?**	kwahnz meh-truhs/kee-**loh**-muh-truhs yah dah-**kee** uh
Which way to ...?	**Per on es va a ...?**	puhr **on** uhs bah ah
Do you speak English?	**Parla anglès?**	**par**-luh an-**glehs**
I don't understand	**No l'entenc.**	noh luhn-**teng**

Useful Words

Could you speak more slowly, please?	**Pot parlar més a poc a poc, si us plau?**	pot par-**lah mehs** pok uh pok sees plah-oo
I'm sorry.	**Ho sento.**	oo **sehn**-too

Useful Words

big	**gran**	gran
small	**petit**	puh-**teet**
hot	**calent**	kah-**len**
cold	**fred**	fred
good	**bo**	boh
bad	**dolent**	doo-**len**
enough	**bastant**	bahs-**tan**
well	**bé**	beh
open	**obert**	oo-**behr**
closed	**tancat**	tan-**kat**
left	**esquerra**	uhs-**kehr**-ruh
right	**dreta**	**dreh**-tuh
straight on	**recte**	**rehk**-tuh
near	**a prop**	uh **prop**
far	**lluny**	**lyoon**yuh
up/over	**a dalt**	uh **dahl**
down/under	**a baix**	uh **bah**-eeshh
early	**aviat**	uhv-**yat**
late	**tard**	tahrt
entrance	**entrada**	uhn-**trah**-thuh
exit	**sortida**	soor-**tee**-thuh
toilet	**lavabos/ serveis**	luh-**vah**-boos sehr-**beh**-ees
more	**més**	mess
less	**menys**	men-yees

Shopping

How much does this cost?	**Quant costa això?**	kwahn kost ehs-**shoh**
I would like ...	**M'agradaria ...**	muh-**grah-thuh-ree**-ah
Do you have?	**Tenen?**	tehn-un
I'm just looking, thank you	**Només estic mirant, gràcies.**	noo-mess ehs-teek mee-**rahn** grah-see-uhs
Do you take credit cards?	**Accepten targes de crèdit?**	ak-**sehp**-tuhn tahr-**zhuhs** duh **kreh**-deet
What time do you open?	**A quina hora obren?**	ah keen-uh oh-ruh **oh**-bruhn
What time do you close?	**A quina hora tanquen?**	ah keen-uh oh -ruh **tan**-kuhn
This one.	**Aquest**	ah-**ket**
That one.	**Aquell**	ah-**kehl**
expensive	**car**	kahr
cheap	**bé de preu/ barat**	beh thuh preh-oo/bah-**rat**
size (clothes)	**talla/mida**	tah-lyah/**mee**-thuh
size (shoes)	**número**	noo-mehr-oo
white	**blanc**	blang
black	**negre**	neh-gruh
red	**vermell**	vuhr-**mel**
yellow	**groc**	grok

green	verd	behrt	room?	lliure?	lyuh-ruh
blue	blau	blah-oo	double	habitació	ah-bee-tuh-see-oh
antique store	antiquari/	an-tee-kwah-ree/	room with	doble amb	doh-bluh am
	botiga	boo-tee-gah/dan-	double bed	llit de	lyeet duh
	d'antiguitats	tee-ghee-tats		matrimoni	mah-tree-moh-nee
bakery	el forn	uhl forn	twin room	habitació	ah-bee-tuh-see-oh
bank	el banc	uhl bang		amb dos llits/	am dohs lyeets/
book store	la llibreria	lah lyee-bruh-		amb llits	s am lyeets in-thee-
		ree-ah		individual	vee-thoo-ahls
butcher's	la carnisseria	lah kahr-nee-suh-	single room	habitació	ah-bee-tuh-see-oh
		ree-uh		individual	een-dee-vee-
pastry shop	la pastisseria	lah pahs-tee-suh-			thoo-ahl
		ree-uh	room with	habitació	ah-bee-tuh-see-oh
chemist's	la farmàcia	lah fuhr-mah-	a bath	amb bany	am bahnyuh
		see-ah	shower	dutxa	doo-chuh
fishmonger's	la peixateria	lah peh-shuh-tuh-	porter	el grum	uhl groom
		ree-uh	key	la clau	lah klah-oo
greengrocer's	la fruiteria	lah froo-ee-tuh-	I have a	Tinc una	ting oo-nuh
		ree-uh	reservation	habitació	ah-bee-tuh-see-oh
grocer's	la botiga de	lah boo-tee-guh duh		reservada	reh-sehr-vah-thah
	queviures	keh-vee-oo-ruhs			
hairdresser's	la perruqueria	lah peh-roo-kuh-	**Eating Out**		
		ree-uh	Have you got a	Tenen	teh-nuhn
market	el mercat	uhl muhr-kat	table for...	taula per...?	tow-luh puhr
newsagent's	el quiosc	uhl kee-ohsk	I would like	Voldria	vool-dree-uh
	de premsa	duh prem-suh	to reserve	reservar	reh-sehr-vahr
post office	l'oficina de	loo-fee-see-nuh	a table.	una taula.	oo-nuh tow-luh
	correus	duh koo-reh-oos	The bill	El compte,	uhl kohm-tuh
shoe store	la sabateria	lah sah-bah-tuh-	please	si us plau.	sees plah-oo
		ree-uh	I am a	Sóc	sok buh-zhuh-tuh-
supermarket	el supermercat	uhl soo-puhr-	vegetarian	vegetarià/	ree-ah
		muhr-kat		vegetariana	buh-zhuh-tuh-
tobacconist's	l'estanc	luhs-tang			ree-ah-nah
travel agency	l'agència de	la-jen-see-uh duh	waitress	cambrera	kam-breh-ruh
	viatges	vee-ad-juhs	waiter	cambrer	kam-breh
			menu	la carta	lah kahr-tuh
Sightseeing			fixed-price	menú del	muh-noo thuhl
art gallery	la galeria d'art	lah gah-luh-ree-	menu	dia	dee-uh
		yuh dart	wine list	la carta de	ah kahr-tuh thuh
cathedral	la catedral	lah kuh-tuh-thrahl		vins	veens
church	l'església	luhz-gleh-zee-uh	glass of water	un got d'aigua	oon got dah-ee-
	la basílica	lah buh-zee-			gwah
		lee-kuh	glass of wine	una copa de vi	oo-nuh ko-pah
garden	el jardí	uhl zhahr-dee			thuh vee
library	la biblioteca	lah bee-blee-oo-	bottle	una ampolla	oo-nuh am-pol-
		teh-kuh			yuh
museum	el museu	uhl moo-seh-oo	knife	un ganivet	oon gun-ee-veht
tourist infor	l'oficina de	loo-fee-see-nuh	fork	una forquilla	oo-nuh foor-keel-
mation office	turisme	thuh too-reez-muh			yuh
town hall	l'ajuntament	luh-djoon-tuh-men	spoon	una cullera	oo-nuh kool-
closed for	tancat per	tan-kat puhr			yeh-ruh
holiday	vacances	bah-kan-suhs	breakfast	l'esmorzar	les-moor-sah
bus station	l'estació	luhs-tah-see-oh	lunch	el dinar	uhl dee-nah
	d'autobusos	dow-toh-boo-zoos	dinner	el sopar	uhl soo-pah
railway	l'estació	luhs-tah-see-oh	main course	el primer plat	uhl pree-meh plat
station	de tren	thuh tren	starters	els entrants	uhlz ehn-tranz
			dish of the day	el plat del dia	uhl plat duhl
Staying in a Hotel					dee-uh
Do you have	¿Tenen una	teh-nuhn oo-nuh	coffee	el cafè	uhl kah-feh
a vacant	habitació	ah-bee-tuh-see-oh	rare	poc fet	pok fet
			medium	al punt	ahl poon
			well done	molt fet	mol fet

Menu Decoder

l'aigua mineral	**lah**-ee-gwuh mee-nuh-**rahl**	mineral water
sense gas/	sen-zuh gas/	still
amb gas	am gas	sparkling
al forn	ahl **forn**	baked
l'all	**lahl**yuh	garlic
l'arròs	lahr-**roz**	rice
les botifarres	lahs **boo**-tee-fah-rahs	sausages
la carn	lah **karn**	meat
la ceba	lah **seh**-buh	onion
la cervesa	lah-sehr-**ve**-sah	beer
l'embotit	lum-boo-**teet**	cold meat
el filet	uhl fee-**let**	sirloin
el formatge	uhl for-**mah**-djuh	cheese
fregit	freh-**zheet**	fried
la fruita	lah froo-**ee**-tah	fruit
els fruits secs	uhlz froo-**eets seks**	nuts
les gambes	lahs **gam**-bus	prawns
el gelat	uhl djuh-**lat**	ice cream
la llagosta	lah lyah-**gos**-tah	lobster
la llet	lah **lyet**	milk
la llimona	lah lyee-**moh**-nah	lemon
la llimonada	lah lyee-moh-**nah**-tuh	lemonade
la mantega	lah mahn-**teh**-gah	butter
el marisc	uhl muh-**reesk**	seafood
la menestra	lah muh-**nehs**-truh	vegetable stew
l'oli	**loll**-ee	oil
les olives	luhs oo-**lee**-vuhs	olives
l'ou	**loh**-oo	egg
el pa	uhl **pah**	bread
el pastís	uhl pahs-**tees**	pie/cake
les patates	lahs pah-**tah**-tuhs	potatoes
el pebre	uhl **peh**-bruh	pepper
el peix	uhl **pehsh**	fish
el pernil	uhl puhr-**neel**	cured ham
salat serrà	suh-**lat** sehr-**rah**	
el plàtan	uhl **plah**-tun	banana
el pollastre	uhl poo-**lyah**-struh	chicken
la poma	la **poh**-mah	apple
el porc	uhl **pohr**	pork
les postres	lahs **pohs**-truhs	dessert
rostit	rohs-**teet**	roast
la sal	lah **sahl**	salt
la salsa	lah **sahl**-suh	sauce
les salsitxes	lahs sahl-**see**-chuhs	sausages
sec	**sehk**	dry
la sopa	lah **soh**-puh	soup
el sucre	uhl-**soo**-kruh	sugar
la taronja	lah tuh-**rohn**-djuh	orange
el te	uhl **teh**	tea
les torrades	lahs too-**rah**-thuhs	toast
la vedella	lah veh-**theh**-lyuh	beef
el vi blanc	uhl **bee blang**	white wine
el vi negre	uhl **bee neh**-gruh	red wine
el vi rosat	uhl **bee roo-zaht**	rosé wine
el vinagre	uhl bee-**nah**-gruh	vinegar
el xai/el be	uhl **shah**ee/uhl beh	lamb
la xocolata	lah shoo-koo-**lah**-tuh	chocolate
el xoriç	uhl shoo-**rees**	red sausage

Numbers

0	zero	**seh**-roo
1	un (masc)	oon
	una (fem)	oon-uh
2	dos (masc)	dohs
	dues (fem)	**doo**-uhs
3	tres	trehs
4	quatre	**kwa**-truh
5	cinc	seeng
6	sis	sees
7	set	set
8	vuit	**voo**-eet
9	nou	noh-oo
10	deu	**deh**-oo
11	onze	**on**-zuh
12	dotze	**doh**-dzuh
13	tretze	**treh**-dzuh
14	catorze	kah-**tohr**-dzuh
15	quinze	**keen**-zuh
16	setze	**set**-zuh
17	disset	dee-**set**
18	divuit	dee-voo-**eet**
19	dinou	dee-**noh**-oo
20	vint	**been**
21	vint-i-un	been-tee-**oon**
22	vint-i-dos	been-tee-**dohs**
30	trenta	**tren**-tah
31	trenta-un	**tren**-tah oon
40	quaranta	kwuh-**ran**-tah
50	cinquanta	seen-**kwahn**-tah
60	seixanta	seh-ee-**shan**-tah
70	setanta	seh-**tan**-tah
80	vuitanta	voo-ee-**tan**-tah
90	noranta	noh-**ran**-tah
100	cent	**sen**
101	cent un	**sent** oon
102	cent dos	**sen** dohs
200	dos-cents (masc)	dohs-**sens**
	dues-centes (fem)	**doo**-uhs sen-tuhs
300	tres-cents	trehs-**senz**
400	quatre-cents	kwah-truh-**senz**
500	cinc-cents	seeng-**senz**
600	sis-cents	sees-**senz**
700	set-cents	set-**senz**
800	vuit-cents	voo-eet-**senz**
900	nou-cents	noh-oo-**cenz**
1,000	mil	**meel**
1,001	mil un	**meel** oon

Time

one minute	un minut	oon mee-**noot**
one hour	una hora	oo-nuh **oh**-ruh
half an hour	mitja hora	**mee**-juh **oh**-ruh
Monday	dilluns	dee-**lyoonz**
Tuesday	dimarts	dee-**marts**
Wednesday	dimecres	dee-**meh**-kruhs
Thursday	dijous	dee-**zhoh**-oos
Friday	divendres	dee-**ven**-druhs
Saturday	dissabte	dee-**sab**-tuh
Sunday	diumenge	dee-oo-**men**-juh